Steps to Success
for Women

Jacqui Brauman

Jacqui Brauman

ISBN: 1533086192
ISBN-13: 978-1533086198

DEDICATION

To my husband, who puts up with my workaholism - it's all for you.

Jacqui Brauman

CONTENTS

Jacqui Brauman

ACKNOWLEDGMENTS

To all the new connections in my life that are helping with my mindset
to keep me motivated to achieve my goals.

FOREWORD

Inspiration to character building and worthy achievement is the key point of this book; its object: to arouse women to awaken dormant ambitions in those who have grown discouraged in the daily struggle, to encourage and stimulate the motivation of those women who are setting out to be successful in their own right, with perhaps neither the networks nor capital other than a determination to get on in the world.

Nothing is so fascinating to a woman with high purpose, life, and energy throbbing through her as stories of men and women who have brought great things to pass. Though these themes are as old as the human race, yet they are ever new, and more interesting to the young than any fiction. The romance of achievement under difficulties, of obscure beginnings and triumphant ends; the story of how great people started, their struggles, their long waitings, amid want and woe, the obstacles overcome, the final triumphs; examples, which explode excuses, of people who have seized common situations and made them great, of those of average capacity who have succeeded by the use of ordinary means, by dint of indomitable will and inflexible purpose: these will most inspire the ambitious youth.

This book was original written by Orison Swett Marden and published in 1897. Copyright has expired and the works are in the public domain, so I have taken the original works and re-written it for modern day women. I've removed as much of the sexism and racism, because the lessons that the original author teaches are eternal. The author teaches that that the most forbidding circumstances cannot repress a longing for knowledge, a yearning for growth; that poverty, humble birth, disability, race or gender, have not been able to bar the progress of people with grit; that poverty has rocked the cradle of the giants who have wrung civilisation from barbarism,

1

and have led the world up from savagery to the Hiltons, the Bransons, and the Trumps.

This book shows that it is the woman with one unwavering aim who cuts her way through opposition and forges to the front; that in this fast-paced age, where everything is pusher or pushed, she who would succeed must hold her ground and push hard; that what are stumbling-blocks and defeats to the weak and vacillating, are but stepping-stones and victories to the strong and determined. The author teaches that every germ of goodness will at last struggle into bloom and fruitage, and that true success follows every right step. Yet, it is important to remember that there is something nobler in an occupation than merely living-getting or money-getting; that a person may make millions and be a failure still; that the hand can never safely reach higher than does the heart.

As a professional woman and business owner myself, I appreciated the original pith, point, and purpose of the words of Mr Marden, so I have aimed to keep the tone to be more suggestive than dogmatic, in a style more practical than elegant, more helpful than ornate, more pertinent than novel. Find the practical lessons in this book that will guide you through your life, through the hard times, to ultimate success.

If you want more guidance and inspiration for a life of purpose and success, please visit my website at HaveItAll.net.au

WANTED: A WOMAN

But nature, with a matchless hand, sends forth her nobly born,
And laughs the paltry attributes of wealth and rank to scorn;
She moulds with care a spirit rare, half human, half divine,
And cries exulting, "Who can make a [woman] like mine?"
ELIZA COOK.

*   *   *

What the world wants now; a woman who will not lose her individuality in a crowd, a woman who has the courage of her convictions, who is not afraid to say "No," though all the world say "Yes."

What the world wants now; a woman who, though she is dominated by a mighty purpose, will not permit one great faculty to dwarf, cripple, warp, or mutilate her womanhood; who will not allow the over-development of one facility to stunt or paralyse her other faculties.

What the world wants now; a woman who is larger than her calling, who considers it a low estimate of her occupation to value it merely as a means of getting a living.

What the world wants now; a woman who sees self-development, education and culture, discipline, character and womanhood, in her occupation.

What the world wants now; a woman who is well balanced, who is not cursed with some little defect or weakness which cripples her usefulness

3

and neutralises her powers. Instead, despite any little defect, this woman does not stop.

What the world wants now; a woman who is symmetrical, and not one-sided in her development, who has not sent all the energies of her being into one narrow specialty, and allowed all the other branches of her life to wither and die. A balanced woman.

What the world wants now; a woman who is broadminded, who does not take half views of things.

What the world wants now; a woman who mixes common sense with her theories, who does not let a college education spoil her for practical, every-day life; a woman who prefers substance to show, who regards her good name as a priceless treasure.

The world wants a woman who is educated all over; whose nerves are brought to their acutest sensibility, whose brain is cultured, keen, incisive, penetrating, broad, liberal, deep; whose hands are deft; whose eyes are alert, sensitive, microscopic, whose heart is tender, broad, magnanimous, true.

The whole world is looking for such a woman. Although there are millions out of employment, yet it is almost impossible to find just the right woman in almost any department of life.

*   *   *

Rousseau, in his celebrated essay on education, says: "According to the order of nature, men being equal, their common vocation is the profession of humanity; and whoever is well educated to discharge the duty of a man cannot be badly prepared to fill any of those offices that have a relation to him. ... Nature has destined us to the offices of human life antecedent to our destination concerning society. To live is the profession I would teach him. When I have done with him, it is true he will be neither a soldier, a lawyer, nor a divine. Let him first be a man; Fortune may remove him from one rank to another as she pleases, he will be always found in his place." A woman can be all these things and more, as women are generally capable of broader thought and deeper understanding of others.

Montaigne says our work is not to train a soul by itself alone, nor a body by itself alone, but to train a whole woman.

*   *   *

One great need of the world today is for men and women who are good animals. To endure the strain of our concentrated civilisation, the coming man and woman must have an excess of animal spirits. They must have a robustness of health. Mere absence of disease is not health. It is the overflowing fountain, not the one half full, that gives life and beauty to the valley below. Only she who is healthy exults in mere animal existence; whose very life is a luxury; who feels a bounding pulse throughout her body, who feels life in every limb, as dogs do when scouring over the field, or as surfers do when gliding over the waves.

Sydney Smith said, "I am convinced that digestion is the great secret of life, and that character, virtue and talents, and qualities are powerfully affected by beef, mutton, pie crust, and rich soups. I have often thought I could feed or starve men into virtues or vices, and affect them more powerfully with my instruments of torture than Timotheus could do formerly with his lyre."

What more glorious than a magnificent womanhood, animated with the bounding spirits of overflowing health?

> "'Tis life, not death for which we pant!
> 'Tis life, whereof our nerves are scant:
> More life and fuller, that we want."

It is a sad sight to see thousands of students graduated every year from our grand institutions, whose object is to make stalwart, independent, self-supporting women, turned out into the world saplings instead of stalwart oaks, "memory-glands" instead of brainy women, helpless instead of self-supporting, sickly instead of robust, weak instead of strong, leaning instead of erect.

The character sympathises with and unconsciously takes on the nature of the body. A peevish, snarling, ailing, gossiping woman cannot develop the vigour and strength of character which is possible to a healthy, robust, happy woman. There is an inherent love in the human mind for wholeness, a demand that women shall come up to the highest standard; and there is an inherent protest or contempt for preventable deficiency. Nature too demands that women be ever at the top of their condition.

* * *

As we stand upon the seashore while the tide is coming in, one wave reaches up the beach far higher than any previous one, then recedes, and for some time none that follows comes up to its mark, but after a while the whole sea is there and beyond it, so now and then there comes a woman head and shoulders above her peers, showing that Nature has not lost her ideal, and after a while even the average woman will overtop the highest wave of womanhood yet given to the world.

*   *   *

Apelles hunted over Greece for many years, studying the fairest points of beautiful women, getting here an eye, there a forehead and there a nose, here a grace and there a turn of beauty, for his famous portrait of a perfect woman which enchanted the world. So the coming woman will be a composite, many in one. She will absorb into herself not the weakness, not the follies, but the strength and the virtues of other types of women. She will be a woman raised to the highest power. She will be self-centred, equipoised, and ever master of herself. Her sensibility will not be deadened or blunted by violation of nature's laws. Her whole character will be impressible, and will respond to the most delicate touches of nature.

What an aid to character building would be the determination of the young woman in starting out in life to consider herself her own bank; that her promises will be accepted as good or bad, and will pass current everywhere or be worthless, according to her individual reputation for honour and veracity; that if she lets a promise go unfulfilled, her bank of character will be suspected; if she lets two or three go unfulfilled, public confidence will be seriously shaken; that if they continue to go to unfulfilled, her reputation will be lost and confidence in her ruined.

If the woman should start out with the fixed determination that every statement she makes shall be the exact truth; that every promise she makes shall be redeemed to the letter; that every appointment shall be kept with the strictest faithfulness and with full regard for other people's time, if she should hold her reputation as a priceless treasure, feel that the eyes of the world are upon her, that she must not deviate a hair's breadth from the truth and right; if she should take such a stand at the outset, she would, come to have almost unlimited credit and the confidence of all, and would have developed into a success.

*   *   *

What constitutes a state?
Not high-raised battlement or laboured mound,
Thick wall or moated gate;

Not cities proud with spires and turrets crowned;
Not bays and broad-armed ports,
Where, laughing at the storm, rich navies ride;
Not starred and spangled courts,
Where low-browed baseness wafts perfume to pride.
No: [wo]men, and high-minded men,
With powers as far above dull brutes endued
In forest, brake, or den,
As beasts excel cold rocks and brambles rude,—
Men who their duties know,
But know their rights, and knowing, dare maintain,
Prevent the long-aimed blow,
And crush the tyrant while they rend the chain.
- WILLIAM JONES.

DARE

The Spartans did not inquire how many the enemy are, but where they are.—AGIS II.

What's brave, what's noble, let's do it after the high Roman fashion, and make death proud to take us.—SHAKESPEARE.

To stand with a smile upon your face against a stake from which you cannot get away—that, no doubt, is heroic. But the true glory is resignation to the inevitable. To stand unchained, with perfect liberty to go away, held only by the higher claims of duty, and let the fire creep up to the heart,—this is heroism.—F. W. ROBERTSON.

*   *   *

When the assembled senate of Rome begged Regulus not to return to Carthage to fulfil an illegal promise, he calmly replied: "Have you resolved to dishonour me? Torture and death are awaiting me, but what are these to the shame of an infamous act, or the wounds of a guilty mind? Slave as I am to Carthage, I still have the spirit of a Roman. I have sworn to return. It is my duty. Let the gods take care of the rest."

*   *   *

The courage which Cranmer had shown since the accession of Mary gave way the moment his final doom was announced. The moral cowardice which had displayed itself in his miserable compliance with the lust and despotism of Henry VIII displayed itself again in six successive recantations

8

by which he hoped to purchase pardon. But pardon was impossible; and Cranmer's strangely mingled nature found a power in its very weakness when he was brought into the church of St. Mary at Oxford on the 21st of March, to repeat his recantation on the way to the stake. "Now," ended his address to the hushed congregation before him,—"now I come to the great thing that troubleth my conscience more than any other thing that ever I said or did in my life, and that is the setting abroad of writings contrary to the truth; which here I now renounce and refuse as things written by a hand contrary to the truth which I thought in my heart, and written for fear of death to save my life, if it might be. And, forasmuch as my hand offended in writing contrary to my heart, my hand therefore shall be the first punished; for if I come to the fire it shall be the first burned." "This was the hand that wrote it," he again exclaimed at the stake, "therefore it shall suffer first punishment;" and holding it steadily in the flame, "he never stirred nor cried till life was gone."

*   *   *

"Oh, if I were only a man!" exclaimed Rebecca Bates, a girl of fourteen, as she looked from the window of a lighthouse at Scituate, Mass., during the War of 1812, and saw a British warship anchor in the harbour.

"What could you do?" asked Sarah Winsor, a young visitor. "See what a lot of them the boats contain, and look at their guns!" and she pointed to five large boats, filled with soldiers in scarlet uniforms, who were coming to burn the vessels in the harbour and destroy the town.

"I don't care, I'd fight," said Rebecca. "I'd use father's old shotgun—anything. Think of uncle's new boat and the sloop! And how hard it is to sit here and see it all, and not lift a finger to help. Father and uncle are in the village and will do all they can. How still it is in the town! There is not a man to be seen."

"Oh, they are hiding till the soldiers get nearer," said Sarah, "then we'll hear the shots and the drum."

"The drum!" exclaimed Rebecca, "how can they use it? It is here. Father brought it home last night to mend. See! the first boat has reached the sloop. Oh! they are going to burn her. Where is that drum? I've a great mind to go down and beat it. We could hide behind the sandhills and bushes."

As flames began to rise from the sloop the ardor of the girls increased.

They found the drum and an old fife, and, slipping out of doors unnoticed by Mrs. Bates, soon stood behind a row of sandhills. "Rub-a-dub-dub, rub-a-dub-dub," went the drum, and "squeak, squeak, squeak," went the fife. The Americans in the town thought that help had come from Boston, and rushed into boats to attack the redcoats. The British paused in their work of destruction; and, when the fife began to play "Yankee Doodle," they scrambled into their boats and rowed in haste to the warship, which weighed anchor and sailed away as fast as the wind would carry her.

*   *   *

A woman's piercing shriek suddenly startled a party of surveyors at dinner in a forest of northern Virginia on a calm, sunny day in 1750. The cries were repeated in quick succession, and the men sprang through the undergrowth to learn their cause. "Oh, sir," exclaimed the woman as she caught sight of a youth of eighteen, but a man in stature and bearing; "you will surely do something for me! Make these friends release me. My boy,— my poor boy is drowning, and they will not let me go!"

"It would be madness; she will jump into the river," said one of the men who was holding her; "and the rapids would dash her to pieces in a moment!"

Throwing on his coat, the youth sprang to the edge of the bank, scanned for a moment the rocks and whirling currents, and then, at sight of part of the boy's dress, plunged into the roaring rapids. "Thank God, he will save my child!" cried the mother, and all rushed to the brink of the precipice; "there he is! Oh, my boy, my darling boy! How could I leave you?" But all eyes were bent upon the youth struggling with strong heart and hope amid the dizzy sweep of the whirling currents far below. Now it seemed as if he would be dashed against a projecting rock, over which the water flew in foam, and anon a whirlpool would drag him in, from whose grasp escape would seem impossible. Twice the boy went out of sight, but he had reappeared the second time, although frightfully near the most dangerous part of the river. The rush of waters here was tremendous, and no one had ever dared to approach it, even in a canoe, lest he should be dashed to pieces. The youth redoubled his exertions. Three times he was about to grasp the child, when some stronger eddy would toss it from him. One final effort he makes; the child is held aloft by his strong right arm, but a cry of horror bursts from the lips of every spectator as boy and man shoot over the falls and vanish in the seething waters below.

"There they are!" shouted the mother a moment later, in a delirium of joy. "See! they are safe! Great God, I thank Thee!" And sure enough they emerged unharmed from the boiling vortex, and in a few minutes reached a low place in the bank and were drawn up by their friends, the boy senseless, but still alive, and the youth almost exhausted. "God will give you a reward," solemnly spoke the grateful woman. "He will do great things for you in return for this day's work, and the blessings of thousands besides mine will attend you." The youth was George Washington.

*   *   *

When General Jackson was a judge and was holding court in a small settlement, a border ruffian, a murderer and desperado, came into the court-room with brutal violence and interrupted the court. The judge ordered him to be arrested. The officer did not dare to approach him. "Call a posse," said the judge, "and arrest him." But they also shrank in fear from the ruffian. "Call me, then," said Jackson; "this court is adjourned for five minutes." He left the bench, walked straight up to the man, and with his eagle eye actually cowed the ruffian, who dropped his weapons, afterwards saying, "There was something in his eye I could not resist."

*   *   *

One of the last official acts of the late President Carnot, of France, was the sending of a medal of the French Legion of Honour to a little American girl, who lives in Indiana. While a train on the Pan Handle Railroad, having on board several distinguished Frenchmen, was bound to Chicago and the World's Fair, Jennie Carey, who was then ten years old, discovered that a trestle was on fire, and that if the train, which was nearly due, entered it a dreadful wreck would take place. Thereupon she ran out upon the track to a place where she could be seen from some little distance. Then she took off her red flannel skirt and, when the train came in view, waved it back and forth across the track. It was seen, and the train stopped. On board of it were seven hundred people, many of whom must have suffered death but for Jennie's courage and presence of mind. When they returned to France, the Frenchmen brought the occurrence to the notice of President Carnot, and the result was the sending of the medal of this famous French society, the purpose of which is the honouring of bravery and merit, wherever they may be found.

*   *   *

Louis IX. of France was captured by the Turks at the battle of Mansoora, during the Seventh Crusade, and his wife Marguerite, with a babe at the breast, was in Damietta, many miles away. The Infidels surrounded the city, and pressed the garrison so hard that it was decided to capitulate. The queen summoned the knights, and told them that she at least would die in armour upon the ramparts before the enemy should become masters of Damietta.

"Before her words they thrilled like leaves
When winds are in the wood;
And a deepening murmur told of men
Roused to a loftier mood."

Grasping lance and shield, they vowed to defend their queen and the cross to the last. Damietta was saved.

*   *   *

Pyrrhus marched to Sparta to reinstate the deposed Cleonymus, and quietly pitched his tents before Laconia, not anticipating resistance. In consternation, the Spartans in council decided to send their women to Crete for safety. But the women met and asked Queen Archidamia to remonstrate. She went to the council, sword in hand, and told the men that their wives did not care to live after Sparta was destroyed.

"We are brave men's mothers, and brave men's wives;
We are ready to do and dare;
We are ready to man your walls with our lives,
And string your bows with our hair."

They hurried to the walls and worked all night, aiding the men in digging trenches. When Pyrrhus attacked the city next day, his repulse was so emphatic that he withdrew from Laconia.

*   *   *

Charles V. of Spain passed through Thuringia in 1547, on his return to Swabia after the battle of Muehlburg. He wrote to Catherine, Countess Dowager of Schwartzburg, promising that her subjects should not be molested in their persons or property if they would supply the Spanish soldiers with provisions at a reasonable price. On approaching Eudolstadt, General Alva and Prince Henry of Brunswick, with his sons, invited themselves, by a messenger sent forward, to breakfast with the Countess, who had no choice but to ratify so delicate a request from the commander of an army. Just as the guests were seated at a generous repast, the Countess was called from the hall and told that the Spaniards were using violence and driving away the cattle of the peasants. Quietly arming all her retinue, she bolted and barred all the gates and doors of the castle, and returned to the banquet to complain of the breach of faith. General Alva told her that such was the custom of war, adding that such trifling disorders were not to be heeded. "That we shall presently see," said Catharine; "my poor subjects must have their own again, or, as God lives, prince's blood for oxen's blood!" The doors were opened, and armed men took the places of the waiters behind the chairs of the guests. Henry changed colour; then, as the best way out of a bad scrape, laughed loudly, and ended by praising the splendid acting of his hostess, and promising that Alva should order the cattle restored at once. Not until a courier returned, saying that the order had been obeyed, and all damages settled satisfactorily, did the armed waiters leave. The Countess then thanked her guests for the honour they had done her castle, and they retired with protestations of their distinguished consideration.

*　　*　　*

The great secret of the success of Joan of Arc was the boldness of her attacks.

Courage in danger is half the battle.—PLAUTUS.

Tender handed stroke a nettle,
And it stings you for your pains;
Grasp it like a man of mettle,
And it soft as silk remains.
AARON HILL.

*　　*　　*

A deep sewer at Noyon, France, had been opened for repairs, and carelessly left at night without covering or lights to warn people of danger. Late at night four men stumbled in, and lay some time before their situation was known in the town. No one dared go to the aid of the men, then unconscious from breathing noxious gases, except Catherine Vassen, a servant girl of eighteen. She insisted on being lowered at once. Fastening a rope around two of the men, she aided in raising them and restoring them to consciousness. Descending again, she had just tied a rope around a third man, when she felt her breath failing. Tying another rope to her long, curly hair, she swooned, but was drawn up with the man, to be quickly revived by fresh air and stimulants. The fourth man was dead when his body was pulled up, on account of the delay from the fainting of Catherine.

*   *   *

A Western paper invited the surviving Union and Confederate officers to give an account of the bravest act observed by each during the Civil War. Colonel Thomas W. Higginson said that at a dinner at Beaufort, S. C., where wine flowed freely and ribald jests were bandied, Dr. Miner, a slight, boyish fellow who did not drink, was told that he could not go until he had drunk a toast, told a story, or sung a song. He replied: "I cannot sing, but I will give a toast, although I must drink it in water. It is 'Our Mothers.'" The men were so affected and ashamed that some took him by the hand and thanked him for displaying courage greater than that required to walk up to the mouth of a cannon.

*   *   *

It takes courage for a young woman to stand firmly erect while others are bowing and fawning for praise and power. It takes courage to wear clothes from Target or Kmart while your comrades dress in new designer gear. It takes courage to remain in honest poverty when others grow rich by fraud. It takes courage to say "No" squarely when those around you say "Yes." It takes courage to do your duty in silence and obscurity while others prosper and grow famous although neglecting sacred obligations. It takes courage to unmask your true self, to show your blemishes to a condemning world, and to pass for what you really are.

It takes courage and pluck to be outvoted, beaten, laughed at, scoffed, ridiculed, derided, misunderstood, misjudged, to stand alone with all the world against you, but we live ridiculously for fear of being thought ridiculous.

The young woman who starts out by being afraid to speak what she thinks will usually end by being afraid to think what she wishes.

How we shrink from an act of our own. We live as others live. Custom or fashion dictates, or your doctor or minister, and they in turn dare not depart from their schools. Dress, living, cars, everything must conform, or be ostracised. Who dares conduct her household or business affairs in her own way?

It takes courage for a woman not to bend the knee to popular prejudice.

It takes courage to refuse to follow custom when it is injurious to her health and morals. To espouse an unpopular cause in Congress requires more courage than to lead a charge in battle. How much easier for a politician to prevaricate and dodge an issue than to stand squarely on her own two feet.

As a rule, eccentricity is a badge of power, but how many women would not rather strangle their individuality than be tabooed? Yet fear is really the only thing to fear.

As the strongest woman has a weakness somewhere, so the greatest hero is a coward somewhere.

If a woman would accomplish anything in this world, she must not be afraid of assuming responsibilities. Of course it takes courage to run the risk of failure, to be subjected to criticism for an unpopular cause, to expose one's self to the shafts of everybody's ridicule, but the woman who is not true to herself, who cannot carry out the sealed orders placed in her hands at her birth, regardless of the world's yes or no, of its approval or disapproval, the woman who has not the courage to trace the pattern of her own destiny, which no other soul knows but her own, can never rise to the true dignity of womanhood. All the world loves courage; youth craves it; they want to hear about it, they want to read about it. The fascination of the "blood and thunder" novels and of the cheap story papers for youth are based upon this idea of courage.

* * *

Bruno, condemned to be burned alive in Rome, said to his judge: "You are more afraid to pronounce my sentence than I am to receive it." Anne Askew, racked until her bones were dislocated, never flinched, but looked her tormentor calmly in the face and refused to abjure her faith.

"We are afraid of truth, afraid of fortune, afraid of death, and afraid of each other," said Emerson. Physicians used to teach that courage depends on the circulation of the blood in the arteries, and that during passion, anger, trials of strength, wrestling or fighting, a large amount of blood is collected in the arteries, and does not pass to the veins. A strong pulse is a fortune in itself.

"Doubt indulged becomes doubt realised." To determine to do anything is half the battle. "To think a thing is impossible is to make it so." Courage is victory, timidity is defeat.

*   *   *

That simple shepherd-lad, David, fresh from his flocks, marching unattended and unarmed, save with his shepherd's staff and sling, to confront the colossal Goliath with his massive armour, is the sublimest audacity the world has ever seen.

*   *   *

Execute your resolutions immediately. Thoughts are but dreams till their effects be tried. Does competition trouble you? Work away; what is your competitor but a man? Conquer your place in the world, for all things serve a brave soul. Combat difficulty gracefully; sustain misfortune bravely; endure poverty nobly; encounter disappointment courageously. The influence of the brave woman is a magnetism which creates an epidemic of noble zeal in all about her. Every day sends to the grave obscure men, who have only remained in obscurity because their timidity has prevented them from making a first effort; and who, if they could have been induced to begin, would, in all probability, have gone great lengths in the career of usefulness and fame. "No great deed is done," says George Eliot, "by falterers who ask for certainty." The brave, cheerful woman will survive her blighted hopes and disappointments, take them for just what they are, lessons and perhaps blessings in disguise, and will march boldly and cheerfully forward in the battle of life. Or, if necessary, she will bear her ills with a patience and calm endurance deeper than ever plummet sounded. She is the true superwoman.

*   *   *

Then to side with Truth is noble when we share her wretched crust,
Ere her cause bring fame and profit, and 't is prosperous to be just;
Then it is the brave man chooses, while the coward stands aside,
Doubting in his abject spirit, till his Lord is crucified.
LOWELL.

Our doubts are traitors,
"And make us lose the good we oft might win,
By fearing to attempt.
SHAKESPEARE.

*   *   *

After the great inward struggle was over, and he had determined to remain loyal to his principles, Thomas More walked cheerfully to the block. His wife called him a fool for staying in a dark, damp, filthy prison when he might have his liberty by merely renouncing his doctrines, as some of the bishops had done. But he preferred death to dishonour. His daughter allowed the power of love to drive away fear. She remained true to her father when all others, even her mother, had forsaken him. After his head had been cut off and exhibited on a pole on London Bridge, the poor girl begged it of the authorities, and requested that it be buried in the coffin with her. Her request was granted, for her death occurred soon.

*　*　*

Don't waste time dreaming of obstacles you may never encounter, or in crossing bridges you have not reached.

No great deed is done
By falterers who ask for certainty.
GEORGE ELIOT.

Fortune befriends the bold.—DRYDEN.

*　*　*

Abraham Lincoln's boyhood was one long struggle with poverty, with little education, and no influential friends. When at last he had begun the practice of law, it required no little daring to cast his fortune with the weaker side in politics, and thus imperil what small reputation he had gained. Only the most sublime moral courage could have sustained him as President to hold his ground against hostile criticism and a long train of disaster; to issue the Emancipation Proclamation; to support Grant and Stanton against the clamour of the politicians and the press; and through it all to do the right as God gave him to see the right. Lincoln never shrank from espousing an unpopular cause when he believed it to be right. At the time when it almost cost a young lawyer his bread and butter to defend the fugitive slave, and when other lawyers had refused, Lincoln would always plead the cause of the unfortunate whenever an opportunity presented. "Go to Lincoln," people would say, when these hounded fugitives were seeking protection; "he's not afraid of any cause, if it's right."

*　*　*

As Salmon P. Chase left the court room after making an impassioned plea for the runaway slave girl Matilda, a man looked at him in surprise and said: "There goes a fine young fellow who has just ruined himself." But in thus ruining himself Chase had taken the first important step in a career in which he became Governor of Ohio, United States Senator from Ohio, Secretary of the United States Treasury, and Chief Justice of the United States Supreme Court.

*   *   *

When General Butler was sent with nine thousand men to quell the New York riots, he arrived in advance of his troops, and found the streets thronged with an angry mob, which had already hanged more than one man to lamp-posts. Without waiting for his men, Butler went to the place where the crowd was most dense, overturned an ash barrel, stood upon it, and began: "Delegates from Five Points, fiends from hell, you have murdered your superiors," and the blood-stained crowd quailed before the courageous words of a single man in a city which Mayor Fernando Wood could not restrain with the aid of police and militia.

*   *   *

"Our enemies are before us," exclaimed the Spartans at Thermopylae. "And we are before them," was the cool reply of Leonidas. "Deliver your arms," came the message from Xerxes. "Come and take them," was the answer Leonidas sent back. A Persian soldier said: "You will not be able to see the sun for flying javelins and arrows." "Then we will fight in the shade," replied a Lacedemonian. What wonder that a handful of such men checked the march of the greatest host that ever trod the earth.

*   *   *

The courageous woman is an example to the intrepid. Her influence is magnetic. She creates an epidemic of grace.

The spirit of courage will transform the whole temper of your life. "The wise and active conquer difficulties by daring to attempt them. Sloth and folly shiver and sicken at the sight of trial and hazard, and make the impossibility they fear."

In speech right gentle, yet so wise; princely of mien,
Yet softly mannered; modest, deferent,
And tender-hearted, though of fearless blood.
EDWIN ARNOLD.

*   *   *

Emin Pasha, the explorer of Africa, was left behind by his exploring party under circumstances that were thought certainly fatal, and his death was reported with great assurance. Early the next winter, as his troop was on its toilsome but exciting way through Central Africa, it came upon a most wretched sight. A party of natives had been kidnapped by the slave-hunters, and dragged in chains thus far toward the land of bondage. But small-pox had set in, and the miserable company had been abandoned to their fate. Emin sent his men ahead, and stayed behind in this camp of death to act as physician and nurse. How many lives he saved is not known, though it is known that he nearly lost his own. The age of chivalry is not gone by. This is as knightly a deed as poet ever chronicled.

*   *   *

A mouse that dwelt near the abode of a great magician was kept in such constant distress by its fear of a cat, that the magician, taking pity on it, turned it into a cat itself. Immediately it began to suffer from its fear of a dog, so the magician turned it into a dog. Then it began to suffer from fear of a tiger. The magician therefore turned it into a tiger. Then it began to suffer from fear of hunters, and the magician said in disgust: "Be a mouse again. As you have only the heart of a mouse, it is impossible to help you by giving you the body of a nobler animal."

*   *   *

Men and women who have dared have moved the world, often before reaching the prime of life. It is astonishing what daring to begin and perseverance have enabled even youths to achieve. Alexander, who ascended the throne at twenty, had conquered the known world before dying at thirty-three. Julius Caesar captured eight hundred cities, conquered three hundred nations, and defeated three million men, became a great orator and one of the greatest statesmen known, and still was a young man. Washington was appointed adjutant-general at nineteen, was sent at twenty-one as an ambassador to treat with the French, and won his first battle as a colonel at twenty-two. Lafayette was made general of the whole French army at twenty. Charlemagne was master of France and Germany at thirty. Condé was only twenty-two when he conquered at Rocroi. Galileo was but eighteen when he saw the principle of the pendulum in the swinging lamp in the cathedral at Pisa. Peel was in Parliament at twenty-one. Gladstone was in Parliament before he was twenty-two, and at twenty-four he was Lord of the Treasury. Elizabeth Barrett Browning was proficient in Greek

19

and Latin at twelve; De Quincey at eleven. Robert Browning wrote at eleven poetry of no mean order. Cowley, who sleeps in Westminster Abbey, published a volume of poems at fifteen. N. P. Willis won lasting fame as a poet before leaving college. Macaulay was a celebrated author before he was twenty-three. Luther was but twenty-nine when he nailed his famous thesis to the door of the bishop and defied the pope. Nelson was a lieutenant in the British Navy before he was twenty. He was but forty-seven when he received his death wound at Trafalgar. Charles the Twelfth was only nineteen when he gained the battle of Narva; at thirty-six, Cortez was the conqueror of Mexico; at thirty-two, Clive had established the British power in India. Hannibal, the greatest of military commanders, was only thirty when, at Cannae, he dealt an almost annihilating blow at the republic of Rome; and Napoleon was only twenty-seven when, on the plains of Italy, he outgeneraled and defeated, one after another, the veteran marshals of Austria.

Equal courage and resolution are often shown by women who have passed the allotted limit of life. Victor Hugo and Wellington were both in their prime after they had reached the age of threescore years and ten. George Bancroft wrote some of his best historical work when he was eighty-five. Gladstone ruled England with a strong hand at eighty-four, and was a marvel of literary and scholarly ability.

Shakespeare says: "He is not worthy of the honeycomb that shuns the hive because the bees have stings."

Many a bright youth has accomplished nothing of worth simply because he did not dare to commence.

Begin! Begin!! Begin!!!

*   *   *

Whatever people may think of you, do that which you believe to be right. Be alike indifferent to censure or praise.—PYTHAGORAS."

There are obstinate and unknown braves who defend themselves inch by inch in the shadows against the fatal invasion of want and turpitude. There are noble and mysterious triumphs which no eye sees, no renown rewards, and no flourish of trumpets salutes. Life, misfortune, isolation, abandonment, and poverty are battlefields which have their heroes.—
VICTOR HUGO.

Who waits until the wind shall silent keep,
Who never finds the ready hour to sow,
Who watcheth clouds, will have no time to reap.
HELEN HUNT JACKSON.

THE WILL AND THE WAY

"The 'way' will be found by a resolute will."

"I will find a way or make one."

"A woman alone can perform the impossible. They can who think they can. Character is a perfectly educated will."

The iron will of one stout heart shall make a thousand quail;
A feeble dwarf, dauntlessly resolved, will turn the tide of battle,
And rally to a nobler strife the giants that had fled.
TUPPER.

*   *   *

At a dinner party given in 1837, at the residence of Chancellor Kent, in New York city, some of the most distinguished men in the country were invited, and among them was a young and rather melancholy and reticent Frenchman. Professor Morse was one of the guests, and during the evening he drew the attention of Mr. Gallatin, then a prominent statesman, to the stranger, observing that his forehead indicated great intellect. "Yes," replied Mr. Gallatin, touching his own forehead with his finger, "there is a great deal in that head of his: but he has a strange fancy. Can you believe it? He has the idea that he will one day be the Emperor of France. Can you conceive anything more absurd?" It did seem absurd, for this reserved Frenchman was then a poor adventurer, an exile from his country, without fortune or powerful connections, and yet, fourteen years later, his idea became a fact,—his dream of becoming Napoleon III. was realised. True, before he accomplished his purpose there were long dreary years of

22

imprisonment, exile, disaster, and patient labor and hope, but he gained his ambition at last. He was not scrupulous as to the means employed to accomplish his ends, yet he is a remarkable example of what pluck and energy can do.

* * *

Mr. Ingram, publisher of the "London Illustrated News," who lost his life on Lake Michigan, walked ten miles to deliver a single paper rather than disappoint a customer, when he began life as a newsdealer at Nottingham, England. Does any one wonder that such a youth succeeded? Once he rose at two o'clock in the morning and walked to London to get some papers because there was no post to bring them. He determined that his customers should not be disappointed. This is the kind of will that finds a way.

* * *

There is scarcely anything in all biography grander than the saying of young Henry Fawcett, Gladstone's last Postmaster-General, to his grief-stricken father, who had put out both his eyes by bird-shot during a game hunt: "Never mind, father, blindness shall not interfere with my success in life." One of the most pathetic sights in London streets, long afterward, was Henry Fawcett, M. P., led everywhere by a faithful daughter, who acted as amanuensis as well as guide to her plucky father. Think of a young man, scarcely on the threshold of active life, suddenly losing the sight of both eyes and yet, by mere pluck and almost incomprehensible tenacity of purpose, lifting himself into eminence, in any direction, to say nothing of becoming one of the foremost men in a country noted for its great men. Most youth would have succumbed to such a misfortune, and would never have been heard from again. But fortunately for the world, there are yet left many Fawcetts, many Prescotts, Parkmans, Cavanaghs.

The courageous daughter who was eyes to her father was herself a marvellous example of pluck and determination. For the first time in the history of Oxford College, which reaches back centuries, she succeeded in winning the post which had only been gained before by great men, such as Gladstone,—the post of senior wrangler. This achievement had had no parallel in history up to that date, and attracted the attention of the whole civilised world. Not only had no woman ever held this position before, but with few exceptions it had only been held by men who in after life became highly distinguished. Who can deny that where there is a will, as a rule, there's a way?

The true way to conquer circumstances is to be a greater circumstance yourself.

Yet, while desiring to impress in the most forcible manner possible the fact that will-power is necessary to success, and that, other things being equal, the greater the will-power, the grander and more complete the success, we cannot indorse the preposterous theory that there is nothing in circumstances or environments. We must temper determination with discretion, and support it with knowledge and common sense, or it will only lead us to run our heads against posts. We must not expect to overcome a stubborn fact by a stubborn will. We merely have the right to assume that we can do anything within the limit of our utmost faculty, strength, and endurance. Obstacles permanently insurmountable bar our progress in some directions, but in any direction we may reasonably hope and attempt to go, we shall find that the obstacles, as a rule, are either not insurmountable or else not permanent. The strong-willed, intelligent, persistent woman will find or make a way where, in the nature of things, a way can be found or made.

Every one knows that there are thousands of young women, both in the city and in the country, of superior ability, who seem to be compelled by circumstances to remain in very ordinary positions for small pay, when others about them are raised by money or family influence into desirable places. In other words, we all know that the best women do not always get the best places: circumstances do have a great deal to do with our position, our salaries, and our station in life.

No, the race is not always to the swift.

Every one knows that there is not always a way where there is a will, that labor does not always conquer all things; that there are things impossible even to she that wills, however strongly; that one cannot always make anything of herself she chooses; that there are limitations in our very natures which no amount of will-power or industry can overcome; that no amount of sun-staring can ever make an eagle out of a crow.

The simple truth is that a will strong enough to keep a woman continually striving for things not wholly beyond her powers will carry her in time very far toward her chosen goal.

*   *   *

The greatest thing a woman can do in this world is to make the most possible out of the stuff that has been given to her. This is success, and there is no other.

While it is true that our circumstances or environments do affect us, in most things they do not prevent our growth. The corn that is now ripe, whence comes it, and what is it? Is it not large or small, stunted wild maize or well-developed ears, according to the conditions under which it has grown? Yet its environments cannot make wheat of it. Nor can our circumstances alter our nature. It is part of our nature, and wholly within our power, greatly to change and to take advantage of our circumstances, so that, unlike the corn, we can rise much superior to our natural surroundings simply because we can thus vary and improve the surroundings. In other words, women can usually build the very road on which she is to run her race.

It is not a question of what some one else can do or become, which every girl should ask herself, but what can I do? How can I develop myself into the grandest possible womanhood?

So far, then, from the power of circumstances being a hindrance to women in trying to build for themselves an imperial highway to fortune, these circumstances constitute the very quarry out of which they are to get paving-stones for the road.

While it is true that the will-power cannot perform miracles, yet that it is almost omnipotent, that it can perform wonders, all history goes to prove. As Shakespeare says:—

"Men at some time are masters of their fates:
The fault, dear Brutus, is not in our stars,
But in ourselves, that we are underlings."

*   *   *

"There is nobody," says a Roman Cardinal, "whom Fortune does not visit once in his life: but when she finds he is not ready to receive her, she goes in at the door, and out through the window." Opportunity is coy. The careless, the slow, the unobservant, the lazy fail to see it, or clutch at it when it has gone. The sharp ladies detect it instantly, and catch it when on the wing.

Show me a woman who is, according to popular prejudice, a victim of bad luck, and I will show you one who has some unfortunate crooked twist of temperament that invites disaster. She is ill-tempered, or conceited, or trifling; lacks character, enthusiasm, or some other requisite for success.

What has chance ever done in the world? Has it built any cities? Has it invented any telephones, any telegraphs? Has it built any steamships, established any universities, any asylums, any hospitals? Was there any chance in Caesar's crossing the Rubicon? What had chance to do with Napoleon's career, with Wellington's, or Grant's, or Von Moltke's? Every battle was won before it was begun. What had luck to do with Thermopylae, Trafalgar, Gettysburg? Our successes we ascribe to ourselves; our failures to destiny.

A woman is not a helpless atom in this vast creation, with a fixed position, and naught to do but obey her own polarity.

Believe in the power of will, which annihilates the sickly, sentimental doctrine of fatalism,—you must but can't, you ought but it is impossible.

*   *   *

The indomitable will, the inflexible purpose, will find a way or make one. There is always room for a woman with drive.

"[S]he who has a firm will," says Goethe, "moulds the world to [her]self."

"People do not lack strength," says Victor Hugo, "they lack will."

Nearly all great people have been remarkable above all things else for their energy of will. Of Julius Caesar it was said by a contemporary that it was his activity and giant determination, rather than his military skill, that won his victories. The girl who starts out in life determined to make the most of her eyes and let nothing escape her which she can possibly use for her own advancement; who keeps her ears open for every sound that can help her on her way, who keeps her hands open that she may clutch every opportunity, who is ever on the alert for everything which can help her to get on in the world, who seizes every experience in life and grinds it up into paint for her great life's picture, who keeps her heart open that she may catch every noble impulse, and everything which may inspire her,—that girl will be sure to make her life successful; there are no "ifs" or "ands" about it. If she has her health, nothing can keep her from final success.

No tyranny of circumstances can permanently imprison a determined will.

The world always stands aside for the determined woman. Will makes a way, even through seeming impossibilities. "It is the half a neck nearer that shows the blood and wins the race; the one march more that wins the campaign: the five minutes more of unyielding courage that wins the fight." Again and again had the irrepressible Carter Harrison been consigned to oblivion by the educated and moral element of Chicago. Nothing could keep him down. He was invincible. A son of Chicago, he had partaken of that nineteenth century miracle, that phoenix-like nature of the city which, though she was burned, caused her to rise from her ashes and become a greater and a grander Chicago, a wonder of the world. Carter Harrison would not down. He entered the Democratic Convention and, with an audacity rarely equaled, in spite of their protest, boldly declared himself their candidate. Every newspaper in Chicago, save the "Times," his own paper, bitterly opposed his election: but notwithstanding all opposition, he was elected by twenty thousand majority. The aristocrats hated him, the moral element feared him, but the poor people believed in him: he pandered to them, flattered them, till they elected him. While we would not by any means hold Carter Harrison up to youth as a model, yet there is a great lesson in his will-power and wonderful tenacity of purpose.

*   *   *

"The general of a large army may be defeated," said Confucius, "but you cannot defeat the determined mind of a peasant."

*   *   *

The poor, deaf pauper, Kitto, who made shoes in the almshouse, and who became the greatest of Biblical scholars, wrote in his journal, on the threshold of manhood: "I am not myself a believer in impossibilities: I think that all the fine stories about natural ability, etc., are mere rigmarole, and that every man may, according to his opportunities and industry, render himself almost anything he wishes to become."

*   *   *

Years ago, a young mechanic took a bath in the river Clyde. While swimming from shore to shore he discerned a beautiful bank, uncultivated, and he then and there resolved to be the owner of it, and to adorn it, and to build upon it the finest mansion in all the borough, and name it in honour of the maiden to whom he was espoused. "Last summer," says a well-known American, "I had the pleasure of dining in that princely mansion, and receiving this fact from the lips of the great shipbuilder of the Clyde." That one purpose was made the ruling passion of his life, and all the energies of his soul were put in requisition for its accomplishment.

*   *   *

Lincoln is probably the most remarkable example on the pages of history, showing the possibilities of our civilisation. From the poverty in which he was born, through the rowdyism of a frontier town, the rudeness of frontier society, the discouragement of early bankruptcy, and the fluctuations of popular politics, he rose to the championship of union and freedom. Lincoln's will made his way. When his friends nominated him as a candidate for the legislature, his enemies made fun of him. When making his campaign speeches he wore a mixed jean coat so short that he could not sit down on it, flax and tow-linen trousers, straw hat, and pot-metal boots. He had nothing in the world but character and friends. When his friends suggested law to him, he laughed at the idea of his being a lawyer. He said he hadn't brains enough. He read law barefoot under the trees, his neighbours said, and he sometimes slept on the counter in the store where he worked. He had to borrow money to buy a suit of clothes to make a respectable appearance in the legislature, and walked to take his seat at Vandalia,—one hundred miles. While he was in the legislature, John F. Stuart, an eminent lawyer of Springfield, told him how Clay had even inferior chances to his, had got all of the education he had in a log schoolhouse without windows or doors; and finally induced Lincoln to study law.

*   *   *

"For Romans, in Rome's quarrels,
"Spared neither land nor gold,
Nor son, nor wife, nor limb nor life,
In the brave days of old."

Invincible determination, and a right nature, are the levers that move the world.—PRESIDENT PORTER.

Perpetual pushing and assurance put a difficulty out of countenance and make a seeming difficulty give way.—JEREMY COLLIER.

*   *   *

Dr. Mathews has well said that "there is hardly a word in the whole human vocabulary which is more cruelly abused than the word 'luck.' To all the faults and failures of men, their positive sins and their less culpable shortcomings, it is made to stand a godfather and sponsor. Go talk with the bankrupt man of business, who has swamped his fortune by wild speculation, extravagance of living, or lack of energy, and you will find that he vindicates his wonderful self-love by confounding the steps which he took indiscreetly with those to which he was forced by 'circumstance', and complacently regarding himself as the victim of ill-luck. Go visit the incarcerated criminal, who has imbued his hands in the blood of his fellow-man, or who is guilty of less heinous crimes, and you will find that, joining the temptations which were easy to avoid with those which were comparatively irresistible, he has hurriedly patched up a treaty with conscience, and stifles its compunctious visitings by persuading himself that, from first to last, he was the victim of circumstances. Go talk with the mediocre in talents and attainments, the weak-spirited man who, from lack of energy and application, has made but little headway in the world, being outstripped in the race of life by those whom he had despised as his inferiors, and you will find that he, too, acknowledges the all-potent power of luck, and soothes his humbled pride by deeming himself the victim of ill-fortune. In short, from the most venial offence to the most flagrant, there is hardly any wrong act or neglect to which this too fatally convenient word is not applied as a palliation."

Success in life is dependent largely upon the willpower, and whatever weakens or impairs it diminishes success. The will can be educated. That which most easily becomes a habit in us is the will. Learn, then, to will decisively and strongly; thus fix your floating life, and leave it no longer to be carried hither and thither, like a withered leaf, by every wind that blows. "It is not talent that men lack, it is the will to labor; it is the purpose, not the power to produce."

It was this insatiable thirst for knowledge which held to his task, through poverty and discouragement, John Leyden, a Scotch shepherd's son. Barefoot and alone, he walked six or eight miles daily to learn to read, which was all the schooling he had. His desire for an education defied the extremest poverty, and no obstacle could turn him from his purpose. He was rich when he discovered a little bookstore, and his thirsty soul would drink in the precious treasures from its priceless volumes for hours, perfectly oblivious of the scanty meal of bread and water which awaited him at his lowly lodging. Nothing could discourage him from trying to improve himself by study. It seemed to him that an opportunity to get at books and lectures was all that any man could need. Before he was nineteen, this poor shepherd boy with no chance had astonished the professors of Edinburgh by his knowledge of Greek and Latin.

*   *   *

Webster was very poor even after he entered Dartmouth College. A friend sent him a recipe for greasing his boots. Webster wrote and thanked him, and added: "But my boots need other doctoring, for they not only admit water, but even peas and gravel-stones." Yet he became one of the greatest men in the world. Sydney Smith said: "Webster was a living lie, because no man on earth could be as great as he looked." Carlyle said of him: "One would incline at sight to back him against the world."

Luck is not God's price for success: that is altogether too cheap.

*   *   *

The mathematician tells you that if you throw the dice, there are thirty chances to one against your turning up a particular number, and a hundred to one against your repeating the same throw three times in succession: and so on in an augmenting ratio. What is luck? Is it, as has been suggested, a blind man's buff among the laws? a ruse among the elements? a trick of Dame Nature? Has any scholar defined luck? any philosopher explained its nature? any chemist shown its composition? Is luck that strange, nondescript fairy, that does all things among men that they cannot account for? If so, why does not luck make a fool speak words of wisdom; an ignoramus utter lectures on philosophy?

Girls should be taught that there is something in circumstances; that there is such a thing as a poor pedestrian happening to find no obstruction in her way, and reaching the goal when a better walker finds the drawbridge up, the street blockaded, and so fails to win the race; that wealth often does place unworthy sons in high positions, that family influence does gain a lawyer clients, a physician patients, an ordinary scholar a good professorship; but that, on the other hand, position, clients, patients, professorships, manager's and superintendent's positions do not necessarily constitute success. She should be taught that in the long run, as a rule, the best woman does win the best place, and that persistent merit does succeed.

There is about as much chance of idleness and incapacity winning real success, or a high position in life, as there would be in producing a Paradise Lost by shaking up promiscuously the separate words of Webster's Dictionary, and letting them fall at random on the floor. Fortune smiles upon those who roll up their sleeves and put their shoulders to the wheel; upon women who are not afraid of dreary, dry, irksome drudgery, women of nerve and grit who do not turn aside for dirt and detail.

Girls should be taught that "she alone is great, who, by a life heroic, conquers fate;" that "diligence is the mother of good luck;" that, nine times out of ten, what we call luck or fate is but a mere bugbear of the indolent, the languid, the purposeless, the careless, the indifferent; that the woman who fails, as a rule, does not see or seize her opportunity. Opportunity is coy, is swift, is gone, before the slow, the unobservant, the indolent, or the careless can seize her.

It has been well said that the very reputation of being strong willed, plucky, and indefatigable is of priceless value. It often cows enemies and dispels at the start opposition to one's undertakings which would otherwise be formidable.

* * *

It is astonishing what people who have come to their senses late in life have accomplished by a sudden resolution.

Arkwright was fifty years of age when he began to learn English grammar and improve his writing and spelling. Benjamin Franklin was past fifty before he began the study of science and philosophy. Milton, in his blindness, was past the age of fifty when he sat down to complete his world-known epic, and Scott at fifty-five took up his pen to redeem an enormous liability. "Yet I am learning," said Michael Angelo, when threescore years and ten were past, and he had long attained the highest triumphs of his art.

Even brains are second in importance to will. The vacillating woman is always pushed aside in the race of life. It is only the weak and vacillating who halt before adverse circumstances and obstacles. A woman with an iron will, with a determination that nothing shall check her career, if she has perseverance and grit, is sure to succeed. We may not find time for what we would like, but what we long for and strive for with all our strength, we usually approximate if we do not fully reach. Hunger breaks through stone walls; stern necessity will find a way or make one.

Success is also a great physical as well as mental tonic, and tends to strengthen the will-power. Strong-willed women, as a rule, are successful women, and great success is almost impossible without it.

A woman who can resolve vigorously upon a course of action, and turns neither to the right nor the left, though a paradise tempt her, who keeps her eyes upon the goal, whatever distracts her, is sure of success. We could almost classify successes and failures by their various degrees of will-power. One talent with a will behind it will accomplish more than ten without it.

*   *   *

I wish it were possible to show the girls of the world the great part that the will might play in their success in life and in their happiness also. The achievements of will-power are simply beyond computation. Scarcely anything in reason seems impossible to the woman who can will strong enough and long enough.

History is full of examples of men and women who have redeemed themselves from disgrace, poverty, and misfortune, by the firm resolution of an iron will. The consciousness of being looked upon as inferior, as incapable of accomplishing what others accomplish; the sensitiveness at being considered a dunce in school, has stung many a girl into a determination which has elevated her far above those who laughed at her. "Whatever you wish, that you are; for such is the force of the human will, that whatever we wish to be seriously, and with a true intention, that we become." While this is not strictly true, yet there is a deal of truth in it.

Were I called upon to express in a word the secret of so many failures among those who started out in life with high hopes, I should say unhesitatingly, they lacked will-power. They could not half will. What is a woman without a will? She is like an engine without steam, a mere sport of chance, to be tossed about hither and thither, always at the mercy of those who have wills. I should call the strength of will the test of a young woman's possibilities. Can she will strong enough, and hold whatever she undertakes with an iron grip? It is the iron grip that takes the strong hold on life. What chance is there in this crowding, pushing, selfish, greedy world, where everything is pusher or pushed, for a young woman with no will, no grip on life? "The truest wisdom," said Napoleon, "is a resolute determination."

*   *   *

"The undivided will
'T is that compels the elements and wrings
A human music from the indifferent air."

32

The education of the will is the object of our existence. For the resolute and determined there is time and opportunity.—EMERSON.

SUCCESS UNDER DIFFICULTIES

Victories that are easy are cheap. Those only are worth having which come as the result of hard fighting.—BEECHER.

Yes, to this thought I hold with firm persistence;
The last result of wisdom stamps it true;
[S]he only earns his freedom and existence
Who daily conquers them anew.
GOETHE.

Little minds are tamed and subdued by misfortunes; but great minds rise above them.—WASHINGTON IRVING

* * *

"Eloquence must have been born with you," said a friend to J. P. Curran. "Indeed, my dear sir, it was not," replied the orator, "it was born some three and twenty years and some months after me." Speaking of his first attempt at a debating club, he said: "I stood up, trembling through every fibre, but remembering that in this I was but imitating Tully, I took courage and had actually proceeded almost as far as 'Mr. Chairman,' when, to my astonishment and terror, I perceived that every eye was turned on me. There were only six or seven present, and the room could not have contained as many more; yet was it, to my panic-stricken imagination, as if I were the central object in nature, and assembled millions were gazing upon me in breathless expectation. I became dismayed and dumb. My friends cried, 'Hear him!' but there was nothing to hear." He was nicknamed "Orator Mum," and well did he deserve the title until he ventured to stare in astonishment at a speaker who was "culminating chronology by the most preposterous anachronisms." "I doubt not," said the annoyed speaker, "that 'Orator Mum' possesses wonderful talents for eloquence, but I would recommend him to show it in future by some more popular method than his silence." Stung by the taunt, Curran rose and gave the man a "piece of his mind," speaking quite fluently in his anger. Encouraged by this success, he took great pains to become a good speaker. He corrected his habit of stuttering by reading favorite passages aloud every day slowly and distinctly, and spoke at every opportunity.

* * *

The poor, scrofulous, and almost blind boy, Samuel Johnson, was taken by his mother to receive the touch of Queen Anne, which was supposed to heal the "King's Evil." He entered Oxford as a servant, copying lectures from a student's notebooks, while the boys made sport of the bare feet showing through great holes in his shoes. Someone left a pair of new shoes at his door, but he was too proud to be helped, and threw them out of the window. He was so poor that he was obliged to leave college, and at twenty-six married a widow of forty-eight. He started a private school with his wife's money; but, getting only three pupils, was obliged to close it. He went to London, where he lived on nine cents a day. In his distress he wrote a poem in which appeared in capital letters the line, "Slow rises worth by poverty depressed," which attracted wide attention. He suffered greatly in London for thirteen years, being arrested once for a debt of thirteen dollars. At forty he published "The Vanity of Human Wishes," in which were these lines:—

"Then mark what ills the scholar's life assail;
Toil, envy, want, the patron and the jail."

When asked how he felt about his failures, he replied: "Like a monument,"—that is, steadfast, immovable. He was an indefatigable worker. In the evenings of a single week he wrote "Rasselas," a beautiful little story of the search for happiness, to get money to pay the funeral expenses of his mother. With six assistants he worked seven years on his Dictionary, which made his fortune. His name was then in everybody's mouth, and when he no longer needed help, assistance, as usual, came from every quarter. The great universities hastened to bestow their degrees, and King George invited him to the palace.

* * *

Of five thousand articles sent every year to "Lippincott's Magazine," only two hundred were accepted. How much do you think Homer got for his Iliad? or Dante for his Paradise? Only bitter bread and salt, and going up and down other people's stairs. In science, the man who discovered the telescope, and first saw heaven, was paid with a dungeon: the man who invented the microscope, and first saw earth, died from starvation, driven from his home. It is very clear indeed that God means all good work and talk to be done for nothing. Shakespeare's "Hamlet" was sold for about twenty-five dollars; but his autograph has sold for much more than five thousand dollars.

During the ten years in which he made his greatest discoveries, Isaac Newton could hardly pay two shillings a week to the Royal Society of which he was a member. Some of his friends wanted to get him excused from this payment, but he would not allow them to act.

There are no more interesting pages in biography than those which record how Emerson, as a child, was unable to read the second volume of a certain book, because his widowed mother could not afford the amount (five cents) necessary to obtain it from the circulating library.

David Livingstone at ten years of age was put into a cotton factory near Glasgow. Out of his first week's wages he bought a Latin Grammar, and studied in the night schools for years. He would sit up and study till midnight unless his mother drove him to bed, notwithstanding he had to be at the factory at six in the morning. He mastered Virgil and Horace in this way, and read extensively, besides studying botany. So eager and thirsty for knowledge was he, that he would place his book before him on the spinning-jenny, and amid the deafening roar of machinery would pore over its pages.

George Eliot said of the years of close work upon her "Romola," "I began it a young woman, I finished it an old woman." One of Emerson's biographers says, referring to his method of rewriting, revising, correcting, and eliminating: "His apples were sorted over and over again, until only the very rarest, most perfect, were left. It did not matter that those thrown away were very good and helped to make clear the possibilities of the orchard, they were unmercifully cast aside." Carlyle's books were literally wrung out of him. The pains he took to satisfy himself of a relatively insignificant fact were incredible. Before writing his essay on Diderot, he read twenty-five volumes at the rate of one per day. He tells Edward Fitzgerald that for the twentieth time he is going over the confused records of the battle of Naseby, that he may be quite sure of the topography.

Great people never wait for opportunities; they make them. Nor do they wait for facilities or favouring circumstances; they seize upon whatever is at hand, work out their problem, and master the situation. A young woman determined and willing will find a way or make one.

Great women have found no royal road to their triumph. It is always the old route, by way of industry and perseverance.

* * *

Although Michael Angelo made himself immortal in three different occupations, his fame might well rest upon his dome of St. Peter as an architect, upon his "Moses" as a sculptor, and upon his "Last Judgment" as a painter; yet we find by his correspondence now in the British Museum, that when he was at work on his colossal bronze statue of Pope Julius II., he was so poor that he could not have his younger brother come to visit him at Bologna, because he had but one bed in which he and three of his assistants slept together.

James Brooks, once the editor and proprietor of the "New York Daily Express," and later an eminent congressman, began life as a clerk in a store in Maine, and when twenty-one received for his pay a hogshead of New England rum. He was so eager to go to college that he started for Waterville with his trunk on his back, and when he was graduated he was so poor and plucky that he carried his trunk on his back to the station when he went home.

When Elias Howe, harassed by want and woe, was in London completing his first sewing-machine, he had frequently to borrow money to live on. He bought beans and cooked them himself. He also borrowed money to send his wife back to America. He sold his first machine for five pounds, although it was worth fifty, and then he pawned his letters patent to pay his expenses home.

There is scarcely a great truth or doctrine but has had to fight its way to public recognition in the face of detraction, calumny, and persecution. "Everywhere," says Heine, "that a great soul gives utterance to its thoughts, there also is a Golgotha."

Nearly every great discovery or invention that has blessed mankind has had to fight its way to recognition, even against the opposition of the most progressive people.

Titian used to crush the flowers to get their colour, and painted the white walls of his father's cottage in Tyrol with all sorts of pictures, at which the mountaineers gazed in wonder. "That boy will beat me one day," said an old painter as he watched a little fellow named Michael Angelo making drawings of pot and brushes, easel and stool, and other articles in the studio. The barefoot boy did persevere until he had overcome every difficulty and become a master of his art.

William H. Prescott was a remarkable example of what a boy with "no chance" can do. While at college, he lost one eye by a hard piece of bread thrown during a "biscuit battle," then so common after meals; and, from sympathy, the other eye became almost useless. But the boy had pluck and determination, and would not lead a useless life. He set his heart upon being a historian, and turned all his energies in that direction. By the aid of others' eyes, he spent ten years studying before he even decided upon a particular theme for his first book. Then he spent ten years more, poring over old archives and manuscripts, before he published his "Ferdinand and Isabella." What a lesson in his life for young men! What a rebuke to those who have thrown away their opportunities and wasted their lives!

*   *   *

Surroundings which women call unfavourable cannot prevent the unfolding of your powers. From the plain fields and lowlands of Avon came the Shakespearean genius which has charmed the world. From among the rock-ribbed hills of New Hampshire sprang the greatest of American orators and statesmen, Daniel Webster. From the crowded ranks of toil, and homes to which luxury is a stranger, have often come the leaders and benefactors of our race. Indeed, when Christ came upon earth, His early abode was a place so poor and so much despised that men thought He could not be the Christ, asking, in utter astonishment, "Can any good thing come out of Nazareth?"

Where shall we find an illustration more impressive than in Abraham Lincoln, whose life, career, and death might be chanted by a Greek chorus as at once the prelude and the epilogue of the most imperial theme of modern times? Born as lowly as the Son of God, in a hovel; of what real parentage we know not, reared in penury, squalor, with no gleam of light, nor fair surrounding; a young manhood vexed by weird dreams and visions; with scarcely a natural grace; singularly awkward, ungainly even among the uncouth about him: it was reserved for this remarkable character, late in life, to be snatched from obscurity, raised to supreme command at a supreme moment, and entrusted with the destiny of a nation. The great leaders of his party were made to stand aside; the most experienced and accomplished men of the day, men like Seward, and Chase, and Sumner, statesmen famous and trained, were sent to the rear, while this strange figure was brought by unseen hands to the front, and given the reins of power.

The story is told of a man in London deprived of both legs and arms, who managed to write with his mouth and perform other things so remarkable as to enable him to earn a fair living. He would lay certain sheets of paper together, pinning them at the corner to make them hold. Then he would take a pen and write some verses; after which he would proceed to embellish the lines by many skilful flourishes. Dropping the pen from his mouth, he would next take up a needle and thread, also with his mouth, thread the needle, and make several stitches. He also painted with a brush, and was in many other ways a wonderful man. Instead of being a burden to his family he was the most important contributor to their welfare.

*   *   *

Arthur Cavanagh, M. P., was born without arms or legs, yet it is said that he was a good shot, a skillful fisherman and sailor, and one of the best cross country riders in Ireland. He was a good conversationalist, and an able member of Parliament. He ate with his fork attached to his stump of an arm, and wrote holding his pen in his teeth. In riding he held the bridle in his mouth, his body being strapped to the saddle. He once lost his means of support in India, but went to work with his accustomed energy, and obtained employment as a carrier of dispatches.

John B. Herreshoff, of Bristol, R. I., although blind since he was fifteen years old, is the founder and head of one of the most noted shipbuilding establishments in the world. He has superintended the construction of some of the swiftest torpedo boats and steam and sailing yachts afloat. He frequently takes his turn at the wheel in sailing his vessels on trial trips. He is aided greatly by his younger brother Nathaniel, but can plan vessels and conduct business without him. After examining a vessel's hull or a good model of it, he will give detailed instructions for building another just like it, and will make a more accurate duplicate than can most boat-builders whose sight is perfect.

Blind Fanny Crosby, of New York, was a teacher of the blind for many years. She has written nearly three thousand hymns, among which are "Pass

Me not, O Gentle Saviour," "Rescue the Perishing," "Saviour more than Life to Me," and "Jesus keep Me near the Cross."

There is no open door to the temple of success. Every one who enters makes her own door, which closes behind her to all others, not even permitting her own children to pass.

*   *   *

Nearly forty years ago, on a rainy, dreary day in November, a young widow in Philadelphia sat wondering how she could feed and clothe three little ones left dependent by the death of her husband, a naval officer. Happening to think of a box of which her husband had spoken, she opened it, and found therein an envelope containing directions for a code of coloured light signals to be used at night on the ocean. The system was not complete, but she perfected it, went to Washington, and induced the Secretary of the Navy to give it a trial. An admiral soon wrote that the signals were good for nothing, although the idea was valuable. For months and years she worked, succeeding at last in producing brilliant lights of different colours. She was paid $20,000 for the right to manufacture them in our navy. Nearly all the blockade runners captured in the Civil War were taken by the aid of the Coston signals, which are also considered invaluable in the Life Saving Service. Mrs. Coston introduced them into several European navies, and became wealthy.

*   *   *

Chauncey Jerome's education was limited to three months in the district school each year until he was ten, when his father took him into his blacksmith shop at Plymouth, Conn., to make nails. Money was a scarce article with young Chauncey. He once chopped a load of wood for one cent, and often chopped by moonlight for neighbours at less than a dime a load. His father died when he was eleven, and his mother was forced to send Chauncey out, with tears in his eyes and a little bundle of clothes in his hand, to earn a living on a farm. His new employer kept him at work early and late chopping down trees all day, his shoes sometimes full of snow, for he had no boots until he was nearly twenty-one. At fourteen he was apprenticed for seven years to a carpenter, who gave him only board and clothes. Several times during his apprenticeship he carried his tools thirty miles on his back to his work at different places. After he had learned his trade he frequently walked thirty miles to a job with his kit upon his back. One day he heard people talking of Eli Terry, of Plymouth, who had undertaken to make two hundred clocks in one lot. "He'll never live long

40

enough to finish them," said one. "If he should," said another, "he could not possibly sell so many. The very idea is ridiculous." Chauncey pondered long over this rumour, for it had long been his dream to become a great clock-maker. He tried his hand at the first opportunity, and soon learned to make a wooden clock. When he got an order to make twelve at twelve dollars apiece he thought his fortune was made. One night he happened to think that a cheap clock could be made of brass as well as of wood, and would not shrink, swell, or warp appreciably in any climate. He acted on the idea, and became the first great manufacturer of brass clocks. He made millions at the rate of six hundred a day, exporting them to all parts of the globe.

*   *   *

"What does he know," said a sage, "who has not suffered?" Schiller produced his greatest tragedies in the midst of physical suffering almost amounting to torture. Handel was never greater than when, warned by palsy of the approach of death, and struggling with distress and suffering, he sat down to compose the great works which have made his name immortal in music. Mozart composed his great operas, and last of all his "Requiem," when oppressed by debt and struggling with a fatal disease. Beethoven produced his greatest works amidst gloomy sorrow, when oppressed by almost total deafness.

Perhaps no one ever battled harder to overcome obstacles which would have disheartened most men than Demosthenes. He had such a weak voice, and such an impediment in his speech, and was so short of breath, that he could scarcely get through a single sentence without stopping to rest. All his first attempts were nearly drowned by the hisses, jeers, and scoffs of his audiences. His first effort that met with success was against his guardian, who had defrauded him, and whom he compelled to refund a part of his fortune. He was so discouraged by his defeats that he determined to give up forever all attempts at oratory. One of his auditors, however, believed the young man had something in him, and encouraged him to persevere. He accordingly appeared again in public, but was hissed down as before. As he withdrew, hanging his head in great confusion, a noted actor, Satyrus, encouraged him still further to try to overcome his impediment. He stammered so much that he could not pronounce some of the letters at all, and his breath would give out before he could get through a sentence. Finally, he determined to be an orator cost what it might. He went to the seashore and practiced amid the roar of the breakers with small pebbles in his mouth, in order to overcome his stammering, and at the same time accustom himself to the hisses and tumults of his audience. He overcame his short breath by practicing speaking while running up steep and difficult places on the shore. His awkward gestures were also corrected by long and determined drill before a mirror.

*   *   *

Columbus was dismissed as a fool from court after court, but he pushed his suit against an incredulous and ridiculing world. Rebuffed by kings, scorned by queens, he did not swerve a hair's breadth from the overmastering purpose which dominated his soul. The words "New World" were graven upon his heart; and reputation, ease, pleasure, position, life itself if need be, must be sacrificed. Threats, ridicule, ostracism, storms, leaky vessels, mutiny of sailors, could not shake his mighty purpose.

You cannot keep a determined person from success. Place stumbling-blocks in her way and she takes them for stepping-stones, and on them will climb to greatness. Take away her money, and she makes spurs of her poverty to urge her on. Cripple her, and she writes the Waverley Novels. Lock her up in a dungeon, and she composes the immortal "Pilgrim's Progress." Put her in a cradle in a log cabin in the wilderness of America, and in a few years you will find her in the Capitol at the head of the greatest nation on the globe.

Would it were possible to convince the struggling girl of today that all that is great and noble and true in the history of the world is the result of infinite pains-taking, perpetual plodding, of common every-day industry!

*   *   *

Roger Bacon, one of the profoundest thinkers the world has produced, was terribly persecuted for his studies in natural philosophy, yet he persevered and won success. He was accused of dealing in magic, his books were burned in public, and he was kept in prison for ten years. Even our own revered Washington was mobbed in the streets because he would not pander to the clamour of the people and reject the treaty which Mr. Jay had arranged with Great Britain. But he remained firm, and the people adopted his opinion. The Duke of Wellington was mobbed in the streets of London and his windows were broken while his wife lay dead in the house; but the "Iron Duke" never faltered in his course, or swerved a hair's breadth from his purpose.

William Phips, when a young man, heard some sailors on the street, in Boston, talking about a Spanish ship, wrecked off the Bahama Islands, which was supposed to have money on board. Young Phips determined to find it. He set out at once, and, after many hardships, discovered the lost treasure. He then heard of another ship, wrecked off Port De La Plata many years before. He set sail for England and importuned Charles II. for aid. To his delight the king fitted up the ship Rose Algier for him. He searched and searched for a long time in vain. He had to return to England to repair his vessel. James II. was then on the throne, and he had to wait for four years before he could raise money to return. His crew mutinied and threatened to throw him overboard, but he turned the ship's guns on them. One day an Indian diver went down for a curious sea plant and saw several cannon lying on the bottom. They proved to belong to the wreck for which he was looking, sunk fifty years before. He had nothing but dim traditions to guide him, but he returned to England with $1,500,000. The King made him High Sheriff of New England, and he was afterward made Governor of Massachusetts Bay Colony.

A constant struggle, a ceaseless battle to bring success from inhospitable surroundings, is the price of all great achievements.

*   *   *

The woman who has not fought her way up to her own loaf, and does not bear the scar of desperate conflict, does not know the highest meaning of success.

The money acquired by those who have thus struggled upward to success is not their only, or indeed their chief reward. When, after years of toil, of opposition, of ridicule, of repeated failure, Cyrus W. Field placed his hand upon the telegraph instrument ticking a message under the sea, think you that the electric thrill passed no further than the tips of his fingers? When Thomas A. Edison demonstrated in Menlo Park that the electric light had at last been developed into a commercial success, do you suppose those bright rays failed to illuminate the inmost recesses of his soul? Edward Everett said: "There are occasions in life in which a great mind lives years of enjoyment in a single moment. I can fancy the emotion of Galileo when, "first raising the newly constructed telescope to the heavens, he saw fulfilled the grand prophecy of Copernicus, and beheld the planet Venus crescent like the moon. It was such another moment as that when the immortal printers of Mentz and Strasburg received the first copy of the Bible into their hands, the work of their divine art; like that when Columbus, through the grey dawn of the 12th of October, 1492, beheld the shores of San Salvador; like that when the law of gravitation first revealed itself to the intellect of Newton; like that when Franklin saw, by the stiffening fibres of the hemp cord of his kite, that he held the lightning in his grasp, like that when Leverrier received back from Berlin the tidings that the predicted planet was found."

"Observe yon tree in your neighbour's garden," says Zanoni to Viola in Bulwer's novel. "Look how it grows up, crooked and distorted. Some wind scattered the germ, from which it sprung, in the clefts of the rock. Choked up and walled round by crags and buildings, by nature and man, its life has been one struggle for the light. You see how it has writhed and twisted,—how, meeting the barrier in one spot, it has laboured and worked, stem and branch, towards the clear skies at last. What has preserved it through each disfavour of birth and circumstances—why are its leaves as green and fair as those of the vine behind you, which, with all its arms, can embrace the open sunshine? My child, because of the very instinct that impelled the struggle,—because the labour for the light won to the light at length. So with a gallant heart, through every adverse accident of sorrow, and of fate, to turn to the sun, to strive for the heaven; this it is that gives knowledge to the strong and happiness to the weak."

*   *   *

I know no such unquestionable badge and ensign of a sovereign mind as that tenacity of purpose which, through all change of companions, or parties, or fortunes, changes never, bates no jot of heart or hope, but wearies out opposition and arrives at its port.—EMERSON.

"Each petty hand
Can steer a ship becalmed; but he that will
Govern her and carry her to her ends, must know
His tides, his currents; how to shift his sails;
What she will bear in foul, what in fair weathers;
What her springs are, her leaks, and how to stop them;
What strands, what shelves, what rocks to threaten her;
The forces and the natures of all winds,
Gusts, storms, and tempests; when her keel plows hell,
And deck knocks heaven; then to manage her
Becomes the name and office of a pilot."

USE OF OBSTACLES

Nature, when she adds difficulties, adds brains.—EMERSON.

Aromatic plants bestow
No spicy fragrance while they grow;
But crushed or trodden to the ground,
Diffuse their balmy sweets around.
GOLDSMITH.

There is no possible success without some opposition as a fulcrum:
force is always aggressive and crowds something.—HOLMES.

Adversity has the effect of eliciting talents which in prosperous
circumstances would have lain dormant.—HORACE.

Possession pampers the mind; privation trains and strengthens it.—
HAZLITT.

"Kites rise against, not with, the wind."

*　　*　　*

"Many and many a time since," said Harriet Martineau, referring to her
father's failure in business, "have we said that, but for that loss of money,
we might have lived on in the ordinary provincial method of ladies with
small means, sewing and economising and growing narrower every year;
whereas, by being thrown, while it was yet time, on our own resources, we
have worked hard and usefully, won friends, reputation, and independence,
seen the world abundantly, abroad and at home; in short, have truly lived

45

instead of vegetating."

*   *   *

Two of the three greatest epic poets of the world were blind,—Homer and Milton; while the third, Dante, was in his later years nearly, if not altogether, blind. It almost seems as though some great characters had been physically crippled in certain respects so that they would not dissipate their energy, but concentrate it all in one direction.

A distinguished investigator in science said that when she encountered an apparently insuperable obstacle, she usually found herself upon the brink of some discovery.

"Returned with thanks" has made many an author. Failure often leads a woman to success by arousing her latent energy, by firing a dormant purpose, by awakening powers which were sleeping. Women of mettle turn disappointments into helps as the oyster turns into pearl the sand which annoys it.

"Let the adverse breath of criticism be to you only what the blast of the storm wind is to the eagle,—a force against her that lifts her higher."

A kite would not fly unless it had a string tying it down. It is just so in life. The woman who is tied down by half a dozen blooming responsibilities and their children will make a higher and stronger flight than the girl who, having nothing to keep her steady, is always floundering in the mud. If you want to ascend in the world tie yourself to somebody.

*   *   *

"It was the severe preparation for the subsequent harvest," said Pemberton Leigh, the eminent English lawyer, speaking of his early poverty and hard work. "I learned to consider indefatigable labor as the indispensable condition of success, pecuniary independence as essential alike to virtue and happiness, and no sacrifice too great to avoid the misery of debt."

*   *   *

When Napoleon's companions made sport of him on account of his humble origin and poverty he devoted himself entirely to books, and soon rising above them in scholarship, commanded their respect. Soon he was regarded as the brightest ornament of the class.

Thousands of women of great native ability have been lost to the world because they have not had to wrestle with obstacles, and to struggle under difficulties sufficient to stimulate into activity their dormant powers. No effort is too dear which helps us along the line of our proper career.

Poverty and obscurity of origin may impede our progress, but it is only like the obstruction of ice or debris in the river temporarily forcing the water into eddies, where it accumulates strength and a mighty reserve which ultimately sweeps the obstruction impetuously to the sea. Poverty and obscurity are not insurmountable obstacles, but they often act as a stimulus to the naturally indolent, and develop a firmer fibre of mind, a stronger muscle and stamina of body. If the germ of the seed has to struggle to push its way up through the stones and hard sod, to fight its way up to sunlight and air, and then to wrestle with storm and tempest, with snow and frost, the fibre of its timber will be all the tougher and stronger.

"If you wish to rise," said Talleyrand, "make enemies."

*   *   *

There is good philosophy in the injunction to love our enemies, for they are often our best friends in disguise. They tell us the truth when friends flatter. Their biting sarcasm and scathing rebuke are often mirrors which reveal us to ourselves. These unkind stings and thrusts are spurs which urge us on to grander success and nobler endeavour. Friends cover our faults and rarely rebuke; enemies drag out to the light all our weaknesses without mercy. We dread these thrusts and exposures as we do the surgeon's knife, but are the better for them. They reach depths before untouched, and we are led to resolve to redeem ourselves from scorn and inferiority.

We are the victors of our opponents. They have developed in us the very power by which we overcome them. Without their opposition we could never have braced and anchored and fortified ourselves, as the oak is braced and anchored for its thousand battles with the tempests. Our trials, our sorrows, and our griefs develop us in a similar way.

The woman who has triumphed over difficulties bears the signs of victory in her face. An air of triumph is seen in every movement.

*   *   *

John Calvin, who made a theology for the seventeenth and eighteenth centuries, was tortured with disease for many years, and so was Robert Hall. The great men who have lifted the world to a higher level were not developed in easy circumstances, but were rocked in the cradle of difficulties and pillowed on hardships.

*　*　*

"Then I must learn to sing better," said Anaximander, when told that the very boys laughed at his singing. Strong characters, like the palm-tree, seem to thrive best when most abused. People who have stood up bravely under great misfortune for years are often unable to bear prosperity. Their good fortune takes the spring out of their energy, as the torrid zone enervates races accustomed to a vigorous climate. Some people never come to themselves until baffled, rebuffed, thwarted, defeated, crushed, in the opinion of those around them. Trials unlock their virtues; defeat is the threshold of their victory.

It is defeat that turns bone to flint; it is defeat that turns gristle to muscle; it is defeat that makes men invincible; it is defeat that has made those heroic natures that are now in the ascendency, and that has given the sweet law of liberty instead of the bitter law of oppression.

Difficulties call out great qualities, and make greatness possible. How many centuries of peace would have developed a Grant? Few knew Lincoln until the great weight of the war showed his character. A century of peace would never have produced a Bismarck. Perhaps Phillips and Garrison would never have been known to history had it not been for slavery.

The best tools receive their temper from fire, their edge from grinding; the noblest characters are developed in a similar way. The harder the diamond, the more brilliant the lustre, and the greater the friction necessary to bring it out. Only its own dust is hard enough to make this most precious stone reveal its full beauty.

The spark in the flint would sleep forever but for friction; the fire in a woman would never blaze but for antagonism. The friction which retards a train upon the track, robbing the engine of a fourth of its power, is the very secret of locomotion. Oil the track, remove the friction, and the train will not move an inch. The moment a woman is relieved of opposition or friction, and the track of her life is oiled with inherited wealth or other aids, that moment she often ceases to struggle and therefore ceases to grow.

"It is this scantiness of means, this continual deficiency, this constant hitch, this perpetual struggle to keep the head above water and the wolf from the door, that keeps society from falling to pieces. Let every woman have a few more dollars than she wants, and anarchy would follow."

*　　*　　*

Suddenly, with much jarring and jolting, an electric car came to a standstill just in front of a heavy truck that was headed in an opposite direction. The huge truck wheels were sliding uselessly round on the car tracks that were wet and slippery from rain. All the urging of the teamster and the straining of the horses in vain,—until the motorman quietly tossed a shovelful of sand on the track under the heavy wheels, then the truck lumbered on its way. "Friction is a very good thing," remarked a passenger.

The philosopher Kant observes that a dove, inasmuch as the only obstacle it has to overcome is the resistance of the air, might suppose that if only the air were out of the way it could fly with greater rapidity and ease. Yet if the air were withdrawn, and the bird should try to fly in a vacuum, it would fall instantly to the ground unable to fly at all. The very element that offers the opposition to flying is at the same time the condition of any flight whatever.

The effort or struggle to climb to a higher place in life has strength and dignity in it, and cannot fail to leave us stronger for the struggle, even though we miss the prize.

*　　*　　*

From an aimless, idle, and useless brain, emergencies often call out powers and virtues before unknown and suspected. How often we see a young woman develop astounding ability and energy after the death of a parent, or the loss of a fortune, or after some other calamity has knocked the props and crutches from under her. The prison has roused the slumbering fire in many a noble mind. "Robinson Crusoe" was written in prison. The "Pilgrim's Progress" appeared in Bedford Jail. The "Life and Times" of Baxter, Eliot's "Monarchia of Man," and Penn's "No Cross, No Crown," were written by prisoners. Sir Walter Raleigh wrote "The History of the World" during his imprisonment of thirteen years. Luther translated the Bible while confined in the Castle of Wartburg. For twenty years Dante worked in exile, and even under sentence of death. His works were burned in public after his death; but genius will not burn.

Take two acorns from the same tree, as nearly alike as possible; plant one on a hill by itself, and the other in the dense forest, and watch them grow. The oak standing alone is exposed to every storm. Its roots reach out in every direction, clutching the rocks and piercing deep into the earth. Every rootlet lends itself to steady the growing giant, as if in anticipation of fierce conflict with the elements. Sometimes its upward growth seems checked for years, but all the while it has been expending its energy in pushing a root across a large rock to gain a firmer anchorage. Then it shoots proudly aloft again, prepared to defy the hurricane. The gales which sport so rudely with its wide branches find more than their match, and only serve still further to toughen every minutest fibre from pith to bark. The acorn planted in the deep forest shoots up a weak, slender sapling. Shielded by its neighbours, it feels no need of spreading its roots far and wide for support.

Take two boys, as nearly alike as possible. Place one in the country away from the hothouse culture and refinements of the city, with only the district school, the Sunday-school, and a few books. Remove wealth and props of every kind; and, if he has the right kind of material in him, he will thrive. Every obstacle overcome lends him strength for the next conflict. If he falls, he rises with more determination than before. Like a rubber ball, the harder the obstacle he meets the higher he rebounds. Obstacles and opposition are but apparatus of the gymnasium in which the fibres of his manhood are developed. He compels respect and recognition from those who have ridiculed his poverty. Put the other boy in a Vanderbilt family. Give him French and German nurses; gratify every wish. Place him under the tutelage of great masters and send him to Harvard. Give him thousands a year for spending money, and let him travel extensively. The two meet. The city lad is ashamed of his country brother. The plain, threadbare clothes, hard hands, tawny face, and awkward manner of the country boy make sorry contrast with the genteel appearance of the other. The poor boy bemoans his hard lot, regrets that he has "no chance in life," and envies the city youth. He thinks that it is a cruel Providence that places such a wide gulf between them. They meet again as men, but how changed! It is as easy to distinguish the sturdy, self-made man from the one who has been propped up all his life by wealth, position, and family influence, as it is for the shipbuilder to tell the difference between the plank from the rugged mountain oak and one from the sapling of the forest. If you think there is no difference, place each plank in the bottom of a ship, and test them in a hurricane at sea.

*　　*　　*

Two highwaymen chancing once to pass a gibbet, one of them exclaimed: "What a fine profession ours would be if there were no gibbets!" "Tut, you blockhead," replied the other, "gibbets are the making of us; for, if there were no gibbets, every one would be a highwayman." Just so with every art, trade, or pursuit; it is the difficulties that scare and keep out unworthy competitors.

*　　*　　*

"Success grows out of struggles to overcome difficulties," says Smiles. "If there were no difficulties, there would be no success. In this necessity for exertion we find the chief source of human advancement,—the advancement of individuals as of nations. It has led to most of the mechanical inventions and improvements of the age."

John Hunter said that the art of surgery would never advance until professional men had the courage to publish their failures as well as their successes.

"[Girls] need to be taught not to expect a perfectly smooth and easy way to the objects of their endeavour or ambition," says Dr. Peabody. "Seldom does one reach a position with which he has reason to be satisfied without encountering difficulties and what might seem discouragements. But if they are properly met, they are not what they seem, and may prove to be helps, not hindrances. There is no more helpful and profiting exercise than surmounting obstacles."

*　　*　　*

It is said that but for the disappointments of Dante, Florence would have had another prosperous Lord Mayor; and the ten dumb centuries continued voiceless, and the ten other listening centuries (for there will be ten of them, and more) would have had no "Divina Commedia" to hear!

It was in the Madrid jail that Cervantes wrote "Don Quixote." He was so poor that he could not even get paper during the last of his writing, and had to write on scraps of leather. A rich Spaniard was asked to help him, but the rich man replied: "Heaven forbid that his necessities should be relieved, it is his poverty that makes the world rich."

A constant struggle, a ceaseless battle to bring success from inhospitable surroundings, is the price of all great achievements.

* * *

We do our best while fighting desperately to attain what the heart covets. Martin Luther did his greatest work, and built up his best character, while engaged in sharp controversy with the Pope. Later in life his wife asks, "Doctor, how is it that whilst subject to Papacy we prayed so often and with such fervour, whilst now we pray with the utmost coldness and very seldom?"

Waters says that the struggle to obtain knowledge and to advance one's self in the world strengthens the mind, disciplines the faculties, matures the judgment, promotes self-reliance, and gives one independence of thought and force of character.

"The gods in bounty work up storms about us," says Addison, "that give mankind occasion to exert their hidden strength, and throw out into practice virtues that shun the day, and lie concealed in the smooth seasons and the calms of life."

The hothouse plant may tempt a pampered appetite or shed a languid odour, but the working world gets its food from fields of grain and orchards waving in the sun and free air, from cattle that wrestle on the plains, from fishes that struggle with currents of river or ocean; its choicest perfumes from flowers that bloom unheeded, and in wind-tossed forests finds its timber for temples and for ships.

* * *

Kossuth called himself "a tempest-tossed soul, whose eyes have been sharpened by affliction."

Benjamin Franklin ran away, and George Law was turned out of doors. Thrown upon their own resources, they early acquired the energy and skill to overcome difficulties.

As soon as young eagles can fly the old birds tumble them out and tear the down and feathers from their nest. The rude and rough experience of the eaglet fits her to become the bold queen of birds, fierce and expert in pursuing her prey.

Almost from the dawn of history, oppression has been the lot of the Hebrews, yet they have given the world its noblest songs, its wisest proverbs, its sweetest music. With them persecution seems to bring prosperity. They thrive where others would starve. They hold the purse-strings of many nations. To them hardship has been "like spring mornings, frosty but kindly, the cold of which will kill the vermin, but will let the plant live."

*   *   *

In one of the battles of the Crimea a cannon-ball struck inside the fort, crashing through a beautiful garden. But from the ugly chasm there burst forth a spring of water which ever afterward flowed a living fountain. From the ugly gashes which misfortunes and sorrows make in our hearts, perennial fountains of rich experience and new joys often spring.

Don't lament and grieve over lost wealth. The Creator may see something grand and mighty which even He cannot bring out as long as your wealth stands in the way. You must throw away the crutches of riches and stand upon your own feet, and develop the long unused muscles of womanhood. God may see a rough diamond in you which only the hard hits of poverty can polish.

Many a woman has never found herself until she has lost her all. Adversity stripped her only to discover her. Obstacles, hardships are the chisel and mallet which shape the strong life into beauty. The rough ledge on the hillside complains of the drill, of the blasting powder which disturbs its peace of centuries: it is not pleasant to be rent with powder, to be hammered and squared by the quarryman. But look again: behold the magnificent statue, the monument, chiseled into grace and beauty, telling its grand story of valour in the public square for centuries.

The statue would have slept in the marble forever but for the blasting, the chiseling, and the polishing. The angel of our higher and nobler selves would remain forever unknown in the rough quarries of our lives but for the blastings of affliction, the chiseling of obstacles, and the sand-papering of a thousand annoyances.

Who has not observed the patience, the calm endurance, the sweet loveliness chiseled out of some rough life by the reversal of fortune or by some terrible affliction.

*   *   *

How many business women have made their greatest strides, have developed their greatest virtues, when the reverses of fortune have swept away everything they had in the world; when disease had robbed them of all they held dear in life. Often we cannot see the angel in the quarry of our lives, the statue of womanhood, until the blasts of misfortune have rent the ledge, and difficulties and obstacles have squared and chiseled the granite blocks into grace and beauty.

Many a woman has been ruined into salvation. The lightning which smote her dearest hopes opened up a new rift in his dark life, and gave her glimpses of herself which, until then, she had never seen.

The grave buried her dearest hopes, but uncovered possibilities in her nature of patience, endurance, and hope which she never dreamed she possessed before.

"Adversity is a severe instructor," says Edmund Burke, "set over us by one who knows us better than we do ourselves, as he loves us better too. He that wrestles with us strengthens our nerves and sharpens our skill. Our antagonist is our helper. This conflict with difficulty makes us acquainted with our object, and compels us to consider it in all its relations. It will not suffer us to be superficial."

Women who have the right kind of material in them will assert their personality, and rise in spite of a thousand adverse circumstances. You cannot keep them down. Every obstacle seems only to add to their ability to get on.

*   *   *

"Under different circumstances," says Castelar, "Savonarola would undoubtedly have been a good husband, a tender father, a man unknown to history, utterly powerless to print upon the sands of time and upon the human soul the deep trace which he has left, but misfortune came to visit him, to crush his heart, and to impart that marked melancholy which characterises a soul in grief, and the grief that circled his brows with a crown of thorns was also that which wreathed them with the splendour of immortality. His hopes were centred in the woman he loved, his heart was set upon a lifetime with her, and when her family finally rejected him, partly on account of his profession, and partly on account of his person, he believed that it was death that had come upon him, when in truth it was immortality."

The greatest women will ever be those who have risen from the ranks. It is said that there are ten thousand chances to one that genius, talent, and virtue shall issue from a farmhouse rather than from a palace.

Adversity exasperates fools, dejects cowards, draws out the faculties of the wise and industrious, puts the modest to the necessity of trying their skill, awes the opulent, and makes the idle industrious. Neither do uninterrupted success and prosperity qualify women for usefulness and happiness. The storms of adversity, like those of the ocean, rouse the faculties, and excite the invention, prudence, skill, and fortitude of the voyager. The martyrs of ancient times, in bracing their minds to outward calamities, acquired a loftiness of purpose and a moral heroism worth a lifetime of softness and security. A woman upon whom continuous sunshine falls is like the earth in summer: she becomes parched and dry and hard and close-grained. Women have drawn from adversity the elements of greatness. If you have the blues, go and see the poorest and sickest families within your knowledge. The darker the setting, the brighter the diamond.

Don't run about and tell acquaintances that you have been unfortunate; people do not like to have unfortunate men for acquaintances.

* * *

Beethoven was almost totally deaf and burdened with sorrow when he produced his greatest works. Schiller wrote his best books in great bodily suffering. He was not free from pain for fifteen years. Milton wrote his leading productions when blind, poor, and sick. "Who best can suffer," said he, "best can do." Bunyan said that, if it were lawful, he could even pray for greater trouble, for the greater comfort's sake.

A German knight undertook to make an immense Aeolian harp by stretching wires from tower to tower of his castle. When he finished the harp it was silent; but when the breezes began to blow he heard faint strains like the murmuring of distant music. At last a tempest arose and swept with fury over his castle, and then rich and grand music came from the wires. Ordinary experiences do not seem to touch some lives—to bring out any poetry, any higher manhood.

Not until the breath of the plague had blasted a hundred thousand lives, and the great fire had licked up cheap, shabby, wicked London, did she arise, phoenix-like, from her ashes and ruin, a grand and mighty city.

* * *

The appeal for volunteers in the great battle of life, in exterminating ignorance and error, and planting high on an everlasting foundation the banner of intelligence and right, is directed to you. Burst the trammels that impede your progress, and cling to hope. Place high thy standard, and with a firm tread and fearless eye press steadily onward.

Not ease, but effort, not facility, but difficulty, makes strong women. Toilsome culture is the price of great success, and the slow growth of a great character is one of its special necessities.

Byron was stung into a determination to go to the top by a scathing criticism of his first book, "Hours of Idleness," published when he was but nineteen years of age. Macaulay said, "There is scarce an instance in history of so sudden a rise to so dizzy an eminence as Byron reached." In a few years he stood by the side of such men as Scott, Southey, and Campbell, and died at thirty-seven, that age so fatal to genius. Many an orator like "stuttering Jack Curran," or "Orator Mum," as he was once called, has been spurred into eloquence by ridicule and abuse.

*   *   *

This is the crutch age. "Helps" and "aids" are advertised everywhere. We have institutes, colleges, universities, television, books, libraries, blogs, websites, magazines, podcasts. Our thinking is done for us. Our problems are all worked out in "explanations" and "keys." Our children are too often tutored through college with very little study. "Short roads" and "abridged methods" are characteristic of the century. Ingenious methods are used everywhere to get the drudgery out of the college course. The news give us our politics, and preachers our religion. Self-help and self-reliance are getting old fashioned. Nature, as if conscious of delayed blessings, has rushed to woman's relief with her wondrous forces, and undertakes to do the world's drudgery and emancipate her from Eden's curse.

But do not misinterpret her edict. She emancipates from the lower only to call to the higher. She does not bid the world go and play while she does the work. She emancipates the muscles only to employ the brain and heart.

The most beautiful as well as the strongest characters are not developed in warm climates, where woman finds her food ready made on trees, and where exertion is a great effort, but rather in a trying climate and on a stubborn soil. It is rugged necessity, it is the struggle to obtain, it is poverty the priceless spur, that develops the stamina of a real woman, and calls the race out of barbarism. Labour found the world a wilderness and has made it a garden.

As the sculptor thinks only of the angel imprisoned in the marble block, so Nature cares only for the man or woman shut up in the human being. The sculptor cares nothing for the block as such; Nature has little regard for the mere lump of breathing clay. The sculptor will chip off all unnecessary material to set free the angel. Nature will chip and pound us remorselessly to bring out our possibilities. She will strip us of wealth, humble our pride, humiliate our ambition, let us down from the ladder of fame, will discipline us in a thousand ways, if she can develop a little character. Everything must give way to that. Wealth is nothing, position is nothing, fame is nothing, womanhood is everything.

Not ease, not pleasure, not happiness, but a real woman, Nature is after.

*   *   *

"Life," says a philosopher, "refuses to be so adjusted as to eliminate from it all strife and conflict and pain. There are a thousand tasks that, in larger interests than ours, must be done, whether we want them or no. The world refuses to walk upon tiptoe, so that we may be able to sleep. It gets up very early and stays up very late, and all the while there is the conflict of myriads of hammers and saws and axes with the stubborn material that in no other way can be made to serve its use and do its work for man. And then, too, these hammers and axes are not wielded without strain or pang, but swung by the millions of toilers who labour with their cries and groans and tears. The thousand rivalries of our daily business, the fiercer animosities when we are beaten, the even fiercer exultation when we have beaten, the crashing blows of disaster, the piercing scream of defeat,—these things we have not yet gotten rid of, nor in this life ever will. Why should we wish to get rid of them? We are here, my brother, to be hewed and hammered and planed in God's quarry and on God's anvil for a nobler life to come." Only the muscle that is used is developed.

*   *   *

There is a strength
Deep bedded in our hearts of which we reck
But little, till the shafts of heaven have pierced
Its fragile dwelling. Must not earth be rent
Before her gems are found?
MRS. HEMANS.

"If what shone afar so grand

57

Turns to ashes in the hand,
On again, the virtue lies
In the struggle, not the prize."

"The hero is not fed on sweets,
"Daily his own heart he eats;
Chambers of the great are jails,
And head-winds right for royal sails."

"So many great
Illustrious spirits have conversed with woe,
Have in her school been taught, as are enough
To consecrate distress, and make ambition
Even wish the frown beyond the smile of fortune."

Then welcome each rebuff,
That turns earth's smoothness rough,
Each sting, that bids not sit nor stand but go.
BROWNING."

ONE UNWAVERING AIM

Life is an arrow—therefore you must know
What mark to aim at, how to use the bow—
Then draw it to the head and let it go.
HENRY VAN DYKE.

The important thing in life is to have a great aim, and to possess the aptitude and perseverance to attain it.—GOETHE.

Concentration alone conquers.—C. BUXTON.

*   *   *

"Why do you lead such a solitary life?" asked a friend of Michael Angelo.

"Art is a jealous mistress," replied the artist; "she requires the whole man." During his labours at the Sistine Chapel, according to Disraeli, he refused to meet any one, even at his own house.

*   *   *

To succeed today a woman must concentrate all the faculties of her mind upon one unwavering aim, and have a tenacity of purpose which means death or victory. Every other inclination which tempts her from her aim must be suppressed.

A woman may starve on a dozen half-learned trades or occupations; she may grow rich and famous upon one trade thoroughly mastered, even though it be the humblest.

All great people have been noted for their power of concentration which makes them oblivious of everything outside their aim. Victor Hugo wrote his "Notre Dame" during the revolution of 1830, while the bullets were whistling across his garden. He shut himself up in one room, locking his clothes up, lest they should tempt him to go out into the street, and spent most of that winter wrapped in a big grey comforter, pouring his very life into his work.

Genius is intensity. Abraham Lincoln possessed such power of concentration that he could repeat quite correctly a sermon to which he had listened in his boyhood. Dr. O. W. Holmes, when an Andover student, riveted his eyes on the book he was studying as though he were reading a will that made him heir to a million.

It is the women who do one thing in this world who come to the front. It is the woman who never steps outside of her specialty or dissipates her individuality.

*   *   *

A one-talent woman who decides upon a definite object accomplishes more than the ten-talent woman who scatters her energies and never knows exactly what she will do. The weakest living creature, by concentrating her powers upon one thing, can accomplish something; the strongest, by dispersing hers over many, may fail to accomplish anything. Drop after drop, continually falling, wears a passage through the hardest rock. The hasty tempest, as Carlyle points out, rushes over it with hideous uproar and leaves no trace behind.

A great purpose is cumulative; and, like a great magnet, it attracts all that is kindred along the stream of life.

Scientists estimate that there is energy enough in less than fifty acres of sunshine to run all the machinery in the world, if it could be concentrated. But the sun might blaze out upon the earth forever without setting anything on fire; although these rays focused by a burning-glass would melt solid granite, or even change a diamond into vapour. There are plenty of women who have ability enough; the rays of their faculties, taken separately, are all right, but they are powerless to collect them, to bring them all to bear upon a single spot. Versatile women, universal geniuses, are usually weak, because they have no power to concentrate their talents upon one point, and this makes all the difference between success and failure.

Chiseled upon the tomb of a disappointed, heart-broken king, Joseph II. of Austria, in the Royal Cemetery at Vienna, a traveler tells us, is this epitaph: "Here lies a monarch who, with the best of intentions, never carried out a single plan."

One talent utilised in a single direction will do infinitely more than ten talents scattered. A thimbleful of powder behind a ball in a rifle will do more execution than a carload of powder unconfined. The rifle-barrel is the purpose that gives direct aim to the powder, which otherwise, no matter how good it might be, would be powerless. The poorest scholar in school or college often, in practical life, far outstrips the class leader or senior wrangler, simply because what little ability she has she employs for a definite object, while the other, depending upon her general ability and brilliant prospects, never concentrates her powers.

*   *   *

It is fashionable to ridicule the woman of one idea, but the women who have changed the front of the world have been women of a single aim. No woman can make her mark on this age of specialties who is not a woman of one idea, one supreme aim, one master passion. The woman who would make herself felt on this bustling planet, who would make a breach in the compact conservatism of our civilisation, must play all her guns on one point. A wavering aim, a faltering purpose, has no place in the twenty-first century. "Mental shiftlessness" is the cause of many a failure. The world is full of unsuccessful women who spend their lives letting empty buckets down into empty wells.

It is the single aim that wins. Women with monopolising ambitions rarely live in history. They do not focus their powers long enough to burn their names indelibly into the roll of honour.

The world always makes way for the woman with a purpose in her.

The woman who succeeds has a firm goal. She fixes her course and adheres to it. She lays her plans and executes them. She goes straight to her goal. She is not pushed this way and that every time a difficulty is thrown in her path; if she can't get over it she goes through it. Constant and steady use of the faculties under a central purpose gives strength and power, while the use of faculties without an aim or end only weakens them. The mind must be focused on a definite end, or, like machinery without a balance-wheel, it will rack itself to pieces.

This age of concentration calls, not for educated women merely, not for talented women, not for geniuses, not for jacks-of-all-trades, but for women who are trained to do one thing as well as it can be done.

* * *

How many young women fail to reach the point of efficiency in one line of work before they get discouraged and venture into something else. How easy to see the thorns in one's own profession or vocation, and only the roses in that of another. A young woman in business, for instance, seeing a physician riding about town in his new car, visiting his patients, imagines that a doctor must have an easy, ideal life, and wonders that she herself should have embarked in an occupation so full of disagreeable drudgery and hardships. She does not know of the years of dry, tedious study which the physician has consumed, the months and perhaps years of waiting for patients, the dry detail of anatomy, the endless names of drugs and technical terms.

Scientists tell us that there is nothing in nature so ugly and disagreeable but intense light will make it beautiful. The complete mastery of one profession will render even the driest details interesting. The consciousness of thorough knowledge, the habit of doing everything to a finish, gives a feeling of strength, of superiority, which takes the drudgery out of an occupation. The more completely we master a vocation the more thoroughly we enjoy it. In fact, the woman who has found her place and become master in it could scarcely be induced, even though she be a farmer, or a carpenter, or grocer, to exchange places with a governor or congressman. To be successful is to find your sphere and fill it, to get into your place and master it. You can find your passion in mastery.

* * *

There is a sense of great power in a vocation after a woman has reached the point of efficiency in it, the point of productiveness, the point where her skill begins to tell and bring in returns. Up to this point of efficiency, while she is learning her trade, the time seems to have been almost thrown away. But she has been storing up a vast reserve of knowledge of detail, laying foundations, forming her acquaintances, gaining her reputation for truthfulness, trustworthiness, and integrity, and in establishing her credit. When she reaches this point of efficiency, all the knowledge and skill, character, influence, and credit thus gained come to her aid, and she soon

62

finds that in what seemed almost thrown away lies the secret of her prosperity. The credit she established as a clerk, the confidence, the integrity, the friendships formed, she finds equal to a large capital when she starts out for herself and takes the highway to fortune; while the young woman who half learned several trades, and got discouraged and stopped just short of the point of efficiency, just this side of success, is a failure because she didn't go far enough; she did not press on to the point at which her acquisition would have been profitable.

In spite of the fact that nearly all very successful women have made a life work of one thing, we see on every hand hundreds of young women flitting about from occupation to occupation, trade to trade, in one thing today and another tomorrow,—just as though they could go from one thing to another by turning a switch, as if they could run as well on another track as on the one they have left, regardless of the fact that no two careers have the same gauge, that every woman builds her own road upon which another's engine cannot run either with speed or safety. This fickleness, this disposition to shift about from one occupation to another, seems to be peculiar to modern life, so much so that, when a young woman meets a friend whom she has not seen for some time, the commonest question to ask is, "What are you doing now?" showing the improbability or uncertainty that she is doing today what she was doing when they last met.

Conversely, some people think that if they "keep everlastingly at it" they will succeed, but this is not so. Working without a plan is as foolish as going to sea without a compass. A ship which has broken its rudder in mid-ocean may "keep everlastingly at it," may keep on a full head of steam, driving about all the time, but it never arrives anywhere, it never reaches any port unless by accident, and if it does find a haven, its cargo may not be suited to the people, the climate, or conditions among which it has accidentally drifted. The ship must be directed to a definite port, for which its cargo is adapted, and where there is a demand for it, and it must aim steadily for that port through sunshine and storm, through tempest and fog. So a woman who would succeed must not drift about rudderless on the ocean of life. She must not only steer straight toward her destined port when the ocean is smooth, when the currents and winds serve, but she must keep her course in the very teeth of the wind and the tempest, and even when enveloped in the fogs of disappointment and mists of opposition.

*   *   *

On the prairies of South America there grows a flower that always inclines in the same direction. If a traveler loses her way and has neither compass nor chart, by turning to this flower she will find a guide on which she can implicitly rely; for no matter how the rains descend or the winds blow, its leaves point to the north. So there are many women whose purposes are so well known, whose aims are so constant, that no matter what difficulties they may encounter, or what opposition they may meet, you can tell almost to a certainty where they will come out. They may be delayed by head winds and counter currents, but they will always head for the port and will steer straight towards the harbour. You know to a certainty that whatever else they may lose, they will not lose their compass or rudder.

Whatever may happen to a woman of this stamp, even though her sails may be swept away and her mast stripped to the deck, though she may be wrecked by the storms of life, the needle of her compass will still point to the North Star of her hope. Whatever comes, her life will not be purposeless. Even a wreck that makes its port is a greater success than a full-rigged ship with all its sails flying, with every mast and rope intact; which merely drifts into an accidental harbour.

To fix a wandering life and give it direction is not an easy task, but a life which has no definite aim is sure to be frittered away in empty and purposeless dreams. "Listless triflers," "busy idlers," "purposeless busybodies," are seen everywhere. A healthy, definite purpose is a remedy for a thousand ills which attend aimless lives. Discontent, dissatisfaction, flee before a definite purpose. An aim takes the drudgery out of life, scatters doubts to the winds, and clears up the gloomiest creeds. What we do without a purpose begrudgingly, with a purpose becomes a delight, and no work is well done nor healthily done which is not enthusiastically done. It is just that added element which makes work immortal.

*　　*　　*

Mere energy is not enough, it must be concentrated on some steady, unwavering aim. What is more common than "unsuccessful geniuses," or failures with "commanding talents"? Indeed, "unrewarded genius" has become a proverb. Every town has unsuccessful educated and talented women. But education is of no value, talent is worthless, unless it can do something, achieve something. Women who can do something at everything, and a very little at anything, are not wanted in this age. Jacks-at-all-trades are at war with the genius of the times.

What this age wants is young men and women who can do one thing without losing their identity or individuality, or becoming narrow, cramped, or dwarfed. Nothing can take the place of an all-absorbing purpose; education will not, genius will not, talent will not, industry will not, will-power will not. The purposeless life must ever be a failure. What good are powers, faculties, unless we can use them for a purpose? A college education, a head full of knowledge, are worth little to the people who cannot use them to some definite end.

The woman without a purpose never leaves her mark upon the world. She has no individuality; she is absorbed in the mass, lost in the crowd, weak, wavering, incompetent. Her outlines of individuality and angles of character have been worn off, planed down to suit the common thought until she has, as a woman, been lost in the throng of humanity.

A woman who would do some great thing in this short life must apply herself to the work with such a concentration of her forces as, to idle spectators, who live only to amuse themselves, looks like insanity.

*   *   *

What a great directness of purpose may be traced in the career of Pitt, who lived—ay, and died—for the sake of political supremacy. From a child, the idea was drilled into him that he must accomplish a public career worthy of his illustrious father. Even from boyhood he bent all his energy to this one great purpose. He went straight from college to the House of Commons. In one year he was Chancellor of the Exchequer; two years later he was Prime Minister of England, and reigned virtually king for a quarter of a century. He was utterly oblivious of everything outside his aim; insensible to the claims of love, art, literature, living and steadily working for the sole purpose of wielding the governing power of the nation. His whole soul was absorbed in the overmastering passion for political power.

It is a great purpose which gives meaning to life, it unifies all our powers, binds them together in one cable; makes strong and united what was weak, separated, scattered.

"Smatterers" are weak and superficial. Of what use is a woman who knows a little of everything and not much of anything? It is the momentum of constantly repeated acts that tells the story. "Let thine eyes look straight before thee. Ponder the path of thy feet and let all thy ways be established. Turn not to the right hand nor to the left." One great secret of St. Paul's power lay in his strong purpose. Nothing could daunt him, nothing intimidate. The Roman Emperor could not muzzle him, the dungeon could not appall him, no prison suppress him, obstacles could not discourage him.

"This one thing I do" was written all over his work. The quenchless zeal of his mighty purpose burned its way down through the centuries, and its contagion will never cease to fire the hearts of men.

There is no grander sight in the world than that of a young woman fired with a great purpose, dominated by one unwavering aim. She is bound to win; the world stands one side and lets her pass; it always makes way for the woman with a will in her. She does not have one half the opposition to overcome that the undecided, purposeless woman has who, like driftwood, runs against all sorts of snags to which she must yield, because she has no momentum to force them out of her way. What a sublime spectacle it is to see a girl going straight to her goal, cutting her way through difficulties, and surmounting obstacles, which dishearten others, as though they were but stepping-stones! Defeat, like a gymnasium, only gives her new power; opposition only doubles her exertions, dangers only increase her courage. No matter what comes to her, sickness, poverty, disaster, she never turns her eye from her goal.

*　　*　　*

"He who follows two hares is sure to catch neither."

"A double-minded man is unstable in all his ways."

Let every one ascertain [her] special business and calling, and then stick to it if [s]he would be successful.—FRANKLIN.

"Digression is as dangerous as stagnation in the career of a young [wo]man in business."

Every [wo]man who observes vigilantly and resolves steadfastly grows unconsciously into genius.—BULWER.

Genius is intensity.—BALZAC.

SOWING AND REAPING

Sow an act, and you reap a habit; sow a habit, and you reap a character; sow a character, and you reap a destiny.—G. D. BOARDMAN.

Just as the twig is bent the tree's inclined.—POPE.

All habits gather, by unseen degrees,
As brooks make rivers, rivers run to seas.
DRYDEN.

Infinite good comes from good habits which must result from the common influence of example, knowledge, and actual experience—morality taught by good morals.—PLATO.

The chains of habit are generally too small to be felt till they are too strong to be broken.—SAMUEL JOHNSON.

*   *   *

In a fable one of the Fates spun filaments so fine that they were invisible, and she became a victim of her cunning, for she was bound to the spot by these very threads.

Deep in the very nature of animate existence is that principle of facility and inclination, acquired by repetition, which we call habit. A woman becomes a slave to her constantly repeated acts; bad or good. In spite of the protests of her weakened will the trained nerves continue to repeat the acts even when the doer abhors them. What she at first chooses, at last compels.

67

People can be as irrevocably chained to their deeds as atoms are chained by gravitation. You can as easily snatch a pebble from gravitation's grasp as you can separate the minutest act of life from its inevitable effect upon character and destiny. It is hard to break habits.

* * *

Professor Bonelli, of Turin, punctured an animal with the tooth of a rattlesnake. The head of this serpent had lain in a dry state for sixteen years exposed to the air and dust, and, moreover, had previously been preserved more than thirty years in spirits of wine. To his great astonishment an hour afterward the animal died. So habits, good or bad, that have been lost sight of for years will spring into a new life to aid or injure us at some critical moment, as kernels of wheat which had been clasped in a mummy's hand four thousand years sprang into life when planted. They only awaited moisture, heat, sunlight, and air to develop them.

The great thing in all education is to make our nervous system our ally instead of our enemy. It is to fund and capitalise our acquisition, and live at ease upon the interest of the fund. For this we must make automatic and habitual, as soon as possible, as many useful actions as we can, and guard against the growing into ways that are likely to be disadvantageous to us, as we would guard against the plague.

Just one little lie to help me out of this difficulty; "I won't count this." Just one little embezzlement; no one will know it, and I can return the money before it will be needed. Just one little indulgence; I won't count it, and a good night's sleep will make me all right again. Just one small part of my work slighted; it won't make any great difference, and, besides, I am usually so careful that a little thing like this ought not to be counted.

But, my friend, it will be counted, whether you will or not; the deed has been recorded with an iron pen, even to the smallest detail. The Recording Angel is no myth; it is found in ourselves. Its name is Memory, and it holds everything. We think we have forgotten thousands of things until mortal danger, fever, or some other great stimulus reproduces them to the consciousness with all the fidelity of photographs. Sometimes all one's past life will seem to pass before him in an instant; but at all times it is really, although unconsciously, passing before him in the sentiments he feels, in the thoughts he thinks, in the impulses that move him apparently without cause.

"Our acts our angels are, or good or ill,
Our fatal shadows that walk by us still."

*   *   *

Humboldt found in South America a parrot which was the only living creature that could speak a word of the language of a lost tribe. The bird retained the habit of speech after his teachers had died.

Caspar Hauser was confined, probably from birth, in a dungeon where no light or sound from the outer world, could reach him. At seventeen he was still a mental infant, crying and chattering without much apparent intelligence. When released, the light was disagreeable to his eyes; and, after the babbling youth had been taught to speak a few words, he begged to be taken back to the dungeon. Only cold and dismal silence seemed to satisfy him. All that gave pleasure to others gave his perverted senses only pain. The sweetest music was a source of anguish to him, and he could eat only his black crust without violent vomiting.

*   *   *

Practically all the achievements of the human race are but the accomplishments of habit. We speak of the power of Gladstone to accomplish so much in a day as something marvellous; but when we analyse that power we find it composed very largely of the results of habit. His mighty momentum has been rendered possible only by the law of the power of habit. He is now a great bundle of habits, which all his life have been forming. His habit of industry no doubt was irksome and tedious at first, but, practiced so conscientiously and persistently, it has gained such momentum as to astonish the world. His habit of thinking, close, persistent, and strong, has made him a power. He formed the habit of accurate, keen observation, allowing nothing to escape his attention, until he could observe more in half a day in London than a score of men who have eyes but see not. Thus he has multiplied himself many times. By this habit of accuracy he has avoided many a repetition; and so, during his lifetime, he has saved years of precious time, which many others, who marvel at his achievements, have thrown away. Gladstone early formed the habit of cheerfulness, of looking on the bright side of things, which, Sydney Smith says, "is worth a thousand pounds a year." This again has saved him enormous waste of energy, as he tells us he has never yet been kept awake a single hour by any debate or business in Parliament. This loss of energy has wasted years of many a useful life, which might have been saved by forming the economising habit of cheerfulness.

The habit of happy thought would transform the commonest life into harmony and beauty. The will is almost omnipotent to determine habits which virtually are omnipotent. The habit of directing a firm and steady will upon those things which tend to produce harmony of thought would produce happiness and contentment even in the most lowly occupations. The will, rightly drilled, can drive out all discordant thoughts, and produce a reign of perpetual harmony. Our trouble is that we do not half will. After a woman's habits are well set, about all she can do is to sit by and observe which way she is going. Regret it as she may, how helpless is a weak woman bound by the mighty cable of habit, twisted from the tiny threads of single acts which she thought were absolutely within her control!

Drop a stone down a precipice. By the law of gravitation it sinks with rapidly increasing momentum. If it falls sixteen feet the first second, it will fall forty-eight feet the next second, and eighty feet the third second, and one hundred and forty-four feet the fifth second, and if it falls for ten seconds it will in the last second rush through three hundred and four feet till earth stops it. Habit is cumulative. After each act of our lives we are not the same person as before, but quite another, better or worse, but not the same. There has been something added to, or deducted from, our weight of character.

*   *   *

In 1880 one hundred and forty-seven of the eight hundred and ninety-seven inmates of Auburn State Prison were there on a second visit. Recidivism rates are similar today. What brings the prisoner back the second, third, or fourth time? It is habit which drives him on to commit the deed which his heart abhors and which his very soul loathes. It is the momentum made up from a thousand deviations from the truth and right, for there is a great difference between going just right and a little wrong. It is the result of that mysterious power which the repeated act has of getting itself repeated again and again.

When a woman was dying from the effects of her husband's cruelty and debauchery from drink she asked him to come to her bedside, and pleaded with him again for the sake of their children to drink no more. Grasping his hand with her thin, long fingers, she made him promise her: "Mary, I will drink no more till I take it out of this hand which I hold in mine." That very night he poured out a tumbler of brandy, stole into the room where she lay cold in her coffin, put the tumbler into her withered hand, and then took it out and drained it to the bottom. How powerless a man is in the presence

70

of a mighty habit, which has robbed him of will-power, of self-respect, of everything manly, until he becomes its slave!

Etherised by the fascinations of pleasure, we are often unconscious of pain while the devil amputates the fingers, the feet and hands, or even the arms and legs of our character. But oh, the anguish that visits the sad heart when the lethe passes away, and the soul becomes conscious of virtue sacrificed, of life lost.

*   *   *

The hardening, deadening power of depraving habits and customs was strikingly illustrated by the Romans. Under Nero, the taste of the people had become so debauched and morbid that no mere representation of tragedy would satisfy them. Their cold-blooded selfishness, the hideous realism of "a refined, delicate, aesthetic age," demanded that the heroes should actually be killed on the stage. The debauched and sanguinary Romans reckoned life worthless without the most thrilling experiences of horror or delight. Tragedy must be genuine bloodshed, comedy, actual shame. When "The Conflagration" was represented on the stage they demanded that a house be actually burned and the furniture plundered. When "Laureolus" was played they demanded that the actor be really crucified and mangled by a bear, and he had to fling himself down and deluge the stage with his own blood. Prometheus must be really chained to his rock, and Dirce in very fact be tossed and gored by the wild bull, and Orpheus be torn to pieces by a real bear, and Icarus was compelled to fly, even though it was known he would be dashed to death. When the heroism of "Mucius Scaevola" was represented, a real criminal was compelled to thrust his hand into the flame without a murmur, and stand motionless while it was being burned. Hercules was compelled to ascend the funeral pyre, and there be burned alive. The poor slaves and criminals were compelled to play their parts heroically until the flames enveloped them.

The pirate Gibbs, who was executed in New York, said that when he robbed the first vessel his conscience made a hell in his bosom; but after he had sailed for years under the black flag, he could rob a vessel and murder all the crew, and lie down and sleep soundly. A man may so accustom himself to error as to become its most devoted slave, and be led to commit the most fearful crimes in order to defend it, or to propagate it.

An Indian once brought up a young lion, and finding him weak and harmless, did not attempt to control him. Every day the lion gained in strength and became more unmanageable, until at last, when excited by

71

rage, he fell upon his master and tore him to pieces. So what seemed to be an "innocent" sin has grown until it strangled him who was once its easy master.

*　　*　　*

Beware of looking at sin, for at each view it is apt to become better looking.

Habit is practically, for a middle-aged person, fate; for is it not practically certain that what I have done for twenty years I shall repeat today? What are the chances for a woman who has been lazy and indolent all her life starting in tomorrow morning to be industrious; or a spendthrift, frugal; a libertine, virtuous; a profane, foul-mouthed man, clean and chaste?

Habit tends to make us permanently what we are for the moment. We cannot possibly hear, see, feel, or experience anything which is not woven in the web of character. What we are this minute and what we do this minute, what we think this minute, will be read in the future character as plainly as words spoken into the phonograph can be reproduced in the future.

Rectitude is only the confirmed habit of doing what is right. Some women cannot tell a lie: the habit of truth telling is fixed, it has become incorporated with their nature. Their characters bear the indelible stamp of veracity. You and I know women whose slightest word is unimpeachable; nothing could shake our confidence in them. There are other women who cannot speak the truth: their habitual insincerity has made a twist in their characters, and this twist appears in their speech.

You reap what you have sown. Those who have sown dunce-seed, vice-seed, laziness-seed, always get a crop. They that sow the wind shall reap the whirlwind.

Habit, like a child, repeats whatever is done before it. Oh, the power of a repeated act to get itself repeated again and again! But, like the wind, it is a power which we can use to force our way in its very teeth as does the ship, and thus multiply our strength, or we can drift with it without exertion upon the rocks and shoals of destruction.

What a great thing it is to "start right" in life. Every young woman can see that the first steps lead to the last, with all except her own. She can see that others are idle and on the road to ruin, but cannot see it in her own case.

There is a wonderful relation between bad habits. They all belong to the same family. If you take in one, no matter how small or insignificant it may seem, you will soon have the whole. A woman who has formed the habit of laziness or idleness will soon be late at her engagements; a woman who does not meet her engagements will dodge, apologise, prevaricate, and lie. I have rarely known a perfectly truthful woman who was always behind time.

"Small habits, well pursued betimes,
May reach the dignity of crimes."

* * *

Plato wrote over his door, "Let no one ignorant of geometry enter here." The greatest value of the study of the classics and mathematics comes from the habits of accurate and concise thought which it induces. The habit-forming portion of life is the dangerous period, and we need the discipline of close application to hold us outside of our studies.

Washington at thirteen wrote one hundred and ten maxims of civility and good behaviour, and was most careful in the formation of all habits. Franklin, too, devised a plan of self-improvement and character building. No doubt the noble characters of these two men, almost superhuman in their excellence, are the natural result of their early care and earnest striving towards perfection.

"Habit," says Montaigne, "is a violent and treacherous schoolmistress. She, by little and little, slyly and unperceived, slips in the foot of her authority, but having by this gentle and humble beginning, with the aid of time, fixed and established it, she then unmasks a furious and tyrannic countenance against which we have no more the courage nor the power so much as to lift up our eyes."

What is put into the first of life is put into the whole of life.

Benedict Arnold was the only general in the Revolution that disgraced his country. He had great military talent, wonderful energy, and a courage equal to any emergency. But Arnold did not start right. Even when a boy he was despised for his cruelty and his selfishness. He delighted in torturing insects and birds that he might watch their sufferings. He scattered pieces of glass and sharp tacks on the floor of the shop he was tending, to cut the feet of the barefooted boys. Even in the army, in spite of his bravery, the soldiers hated him, and the officers dared not trust him.

"Rogues differ little. Each began as a disobedient son."

* * *

Years ago there was a district lying near Westminster Abbey, London, called the "Devil's Acre,"—a school for vicious habits, where depravity was universal; where professional beggars were fitted with all the appliances of imposture; where there was an agency for the hire of children to be carried about by forlorn widows and deserted wives, to move the compassion of street-giving benevolence; where young pickpockets were trained in the art and mystery which was to conduct them in due course to an expensive voyage for the good of their country to Botany Bay.

Victor Hugo describes a strange association of men in the seventeenth century who bought children and distorted and made monstrosities of them to amuse the nobility with; and in cultured Boston there is an association of so-called "respectable men," who have opened thousands of "places of business" for deforming men, women, and children's souls. But we deform ourselves with agencies so pleasant that we think we are having a good time, until we become so changed and enslaved that we scarcely recognise ourselves. Vice, the pleasant guest which we first invited into our heart's parlour, becomes vulgarly familiar, and entrenches herself deep in our very being. We ask her to leave, but she simply laughs at us from the hideous wrinkles she has made in our faces, and refuses to go. Our secret sins defy us from the hideous furrows they have cut in our cheeks. Each impure thought has chiseled its autograph deep into the forehead, too deep for erasure, and the glassy, bleary eye adds its testimony to our ruined character.

* * *

We scatter seeds with careless hand,
And dream we ne'er shall see them more;
But for a thousand years
Their fruit appears,
In weeds that mar the land.
JOHN KEBLE.

"How shall I a habit break?"
As you did that habit make.
As you gathered, you must lose;
As you yielded, now refuse.

Thread by thread the strands we twist
Till they bind us neck and wrist.
Thread by thread the patient hand
Must untwine ere free we stand.
As we builded, stone by stone,
We must toil, unhelped, alone,
Till the wall is overthrown.

But remember, as we try,
Lighter every test goes by;
Wading in, the stream grows deep
Toward the centre's downward sweep;
Backward turn, each step ashore
Shallower is than that before.

Ah, the precious years we waste
Leveling what we raised in haste;
Doing what must be undone,
Ere content or love be won!
First across the gulf we cast
Kite-borne threads till lines are passed,
And habit builds the bridge at last.
JOHN BOYLE O'REILLY.

SELF HELP

What I am I have made myself.—HUMPHRY DAVY.

God gives every bird its food, but he does not throw it into the nest.—J. G. HOLLAND.

Never forget that others will depend upon you, and that you cannot depend upon them.—DUMAS, FILS.

Our remedies oft in ourselves do lie, which we ascribe to Heaven.— SHAKESPEARE.

Every person has two educations, one which he receives from others, and one, more important, which he gives himself.—GIBBON.

What the superior man seeks is in himself: what the small man seeks is in others.—CONFUCIUS.

In battle or business, whatever the game,
In law, or in love, it's ever the same:
In the struggle for power, or scramble for pelf,
Let this be your motto, "Rely on yourself."
SAXE.

* * *

"Colonel Crockett makes room for himself!" exclaimed a backwoods congressman in answer to the exclamation of the White House usher to

"Make room for Colonel Crockett!" This remarkable man was not afraid to oppose the head of a great nation. He preferred being right to being president. Though rough, uncultured, and uncouth, Crockett was a man of great courage and determination.

Garfield was the youngest member of the House of Representatives when he entered, but he had not been in his seat sixty days before his ability was recognised and his place conceded. He stepped to the front with the confidence of one who belonged there. He succeeded because all the world in concert could not have kept him in the background, and because when once in the front he played his part with an intrepidity and a commanding ease that were but the outward evidences of the immense reserves of energy on which it was in his power to draw.

*　　*　　*

"Take the place and attitude which belong to you," says Emerson, "and all men acquiesce. The world must be just. It leaves every man with profound unconcern to set his own rate."

*　　*　　*

Grant was no book soldier. Some of his victories were contrary to all instructions in military works. He did not dare to disclose his plan to invest Vicksburg, and he even cut off all communication on the Mississippi River for seven days that no orders could reach him from General Halleck, his superior officer; for he knew that Halleck went by books, and he was proceeding contrary to all military theories. He was making a greater military history than had ever been written up to that time. He was greater than all books of tactics. The consciousness of power is everything. That man is strongest who owes most to himself.

Richard Arkwright, the thirteenth child, in a hovel, with no education, no chance, gave his spinning model to the world, and put a sceptre in England's right hand such as the queen never wielded.

"A person under the firm persuasion that he can command resources virtually has them," says Livy.

When asked to name his family coat-of-arms, a self-made President of the United States replied, "A pair of shirtsleeves."

"Poverty is uncomfortable, as I can testify," said James A. Garfield; "but nine times out of ten the best thing that can happen to a young person is to be tossed overboard and compelled to sink or swim. In all my acquaintance I have never known a person to be drowned who was worth the saving."

* * *

To such women, every possible goal is accessible, and honest ambition has no height that genius or talent may tread, which has not felt the impress of their feet.

You may leave your millions to your children, but have you really given them anything? You cannot transfer the discipline, the experience, the power which the acquisition has given you; you cannot transfer the delight of achieving, the joy felt only in growth, the pride of acquisition, the character which trained habits of accuracy, method, promptness, patience, dispatch, honesty of dealing, politeness of manner have developed. You cannot transfer the skill, sagacity, prudence, foresight, which lie concealed in your wealth. It meant a great deal for you, but means nothing to your heir. In climbing to your fortune, you developed the muscle, stamina, and strength which enabled you to maintain your lofty position, to keep your millions intact. You had the power which comes only from experience, and which alone enables you to stand firm on your dizzy height. Your fortune was experience to you, joy, growth, discipline, and character; to your children it will be a temptation, an anxiety, which will probably dwarf them. It was wings to you, it will be a dead weight to them; it was education to you and expansion of your highest powers; to them it may mean inaction, lethargy, indolence, weakness, ignorance. You have taken the priceless spur—necessity—away from them, the spur which has goaded people to nearly all the great achievements in the history of the world.

You thought it a kindness to deprive yourself in order that your children might begin where you left off. You thought to spare them the drudgery, the hardships, the deprivations, the lack of opportunities, the meagre education, which you had on the old farm. But you have put a crutch into their hand instead of a staff; you have taken away from them the incentive to self-development, to self-elevation, to self-discipline and self-help, without which no real success, no real happiness, no great character is ever possible. Their enthusiasm will evaporate, their energy will be dissipated, their ambition, not being stimulated by the struggle for self-elevation, will gradually die away. If you do everything for your children and fight their battles for them, you will have a weakling on your hands.

Those who have been bolstered up all their lives are seldom good for anything in a crisis. When misfortune comes, they look around for somebody to lean upon. If the prop is not there down they go. Once down, they are as helpless as capsized turtles, or unhorsed men in armour. Many a child from poverty has succeeded beyond all their expectations simply because all props were knocked out from under them and they were obliged to stand upon their own feet.

What you call "no chance" may be your "only chance." Don't wait for your place to be made for you; make it yourself. Don't wait for somebody to give you a lift; lift yourself. "Physiologists tell us," says Waters, "that it takes twenty-eight years for the brain to attain its full development. If this is so, why should not one be able, by his own efforts, to give this long-growing organ a particular bent, a peculiar character? Why should the will not be brought to bear upon the formation of the brain as well as of the backbone?" The will is merely our steam power, and we may put it to any work we please. It will do our bidding, whether it be building up a character, or tearing it down. It may be applied to building up a habit of truthfulness and honesty, or of falsehood and dishonour. It will help build up a man or a brute, a hero or a coward. It will brace up resolution until one may almost perform miracles, or it may be dissipated in irresolution and inaction until life is a wreck. It will hold you to your task until you have formed a powerful habit of industry and application, until idleness and inaction are painful, or it will lead you into indolence and listlessness until every effort will be disagreeable and success impossible.

* * *

"The first thing I have to impress upon you is," says J. T. Davidson, "that a good name must be the fruit of one's own exertion. You cannot possess it by patrimony; you cannot purchase it with money; you will not light on it by chance; it is independent of birth, station, talents, and wealth; it must be the outcome of your own endeavour, and the reward of good principles and honourable conduct. Of all the elements of success in life none is more vital than self-reliance,—a determination to be, under God, the creator of your own reputation and advancement. If difficulties stand in the way, if exceptional disadvantages oppose you, all the better, as long as you have pluck to fight through them; it is commonly those who have a tough battle to begin with that make their mark upon their age."

* * *

A young man stood listlessly watching some anglers on a bridge. He was poor and dejected. At length, approaching a basket filled with fish, he sighed, "If now I had these I would be happy. I could sell them and buy food and lodgings." "I will give you just as many and just as good," said the owner, who chanced to overhear his words, "if you will do me a trifling favour." "And what is that?" asked the other. "Only to tend this line till I come back; I wish to go on a short errand." The proposal was gladly accepted. The old man was gone so long that the young man began to get impatient. Meanwhile the fish snapped greedily at the hook, and he lost all his depression in the excitement of pulling them in. When the owner returned he had caught a large number. Counting out from them as many as were in the basket, and presenting them to the youth, the old fisherman said, "I fulfil my promise from the fish you have caught, to teach you whenever you see others earning what you need to waste no time in foolish wishing, but cast a line for yourself."

A white squall caught a party of tourists on a lake in Scotland, and threatened to capsize the boat. When it seemed that the crisis was really come the largest and strongest man in the party, in a state of intense fear, said, "Let us pray." "No, no, my man," shouted the bluff old boatman; "let the little man pray. You take an oar."

The grandest fortunes ever accumulated or possessed on earth were and are the fruit of endeavour that had no capital to begin with save energy, intellect, and the will. From Croesus down to Rockefeller the story is the same, not only in the getting of wealth, but also in the acquirement of eminence; those people have won most who relied most upon themselves.

"It is interesting to notice how some minds seem almost to create themselves," says Irving, "springing up under every disadvantage, and working their solitary but irresistible way through a thousand obstacles."

*   *   *

A woman is not merely the architect of her own fortune, but she must lay the bricks herself. Bayard Taylor, at twenty-three, wrote: "I will become the sculptor of my own mind's statue." His biography shows how often the chisel and hammer were in his hands to shape himself into his ideal. "I have seen none, known none, of the celebrities of my time," said Samuel Cox. "All my energy was directed upon one end, to improve myself."

When young Professor Tyndall was in the government service, he had no definite aim in life until one day a government official asked him how he employed his leisure time. "You have five hours a day at your disposal," said he, "and this ought to be devoted to systematic study. Had I at your age some one to advise me as I now advise you, instead of being in a subordinate position, I might have been at the head of my department." The very next day young Tyndall began a regular course of study, and went to the University of Marburg, where he became noted for his indomitable industry. He was so poor that he bought a cask, and cut it open for a bathtub. He often rose before daylight to study, while the world was slumbering about him.

Labour is the only legal tender in the world to true success. The gods sell everything for that, nothing without it. You will never find success "marked down." The door to the temple of success is never left open. Every one who enters makes his own door which closes behind him to all others.

Circumstances have rarely favoured great women. They have fought their way to triumph over the road of difficulty and through all sorts of opposition. A lowly beginning and a humble origin are no bar to a great career. Our poor boys and girls have written many of our greatest books, and have filled the highest places. Ask almost any great woman in our large cities where she was born, and she will tell you it was on a farm or in a small country town. Nearly all of the great capitalists of the city came from the country. "'T is better to be lowly born."

*　　*　　*

The founder of Boston University left Cape Cod for Boston to make his way with a capital of only four dollars. Like Horace Greeley, he could find no opening for a boy; but what of that? He made an opening. He found a board, and made it into an oyster stand on the street corner. He borrowed a wheelbarrow, and went three miles to an oyster smack, bought three bushels of oysters, and wheeled them to his stand. Soon his little savings amounted to $130, and then he bought a horse and cart. This poor boy with no chance kept right on till he became the millionaire Isaac Rich.

Self-help has accomplished about all the great things of the world. How many young women falter, faint, and dally with their purpose because they have no capital to start with, and wait and wait for some good luck to give them a lift. But success is the child of drudgery and perseverance. It cannot be coaxed or bribed; pay the price and it is yours.

If the girls of today who are struggling against cruel circumstances, to do something and be somebody in the world, could only understand that ninety percent of what is called genius is merely the result of persistent, determined industry, is in most cases downright hard work, that it is the slavery to a single idea which has given to many a mediocre talent the reputation of being a genius, they would be inspired with new hope. It is interesting to note that the men who talk most about genius are the men who like to work the least. The lazier the man, the more he will have to say about great things being done by genius.

The greatest geniuses have been the greatest workers.

*   *   *

Genius has been well defined as the infinite capacity for taking pains. If women who have done great things could only reveal to the struggling girls of today how much of their reputations was due to downright hard digging and plodding, what an uplift of inspiration and encouragement they would give. How often I have wished that the discouraged, struggling girl could know of the heartaches, the headaches, the disheartening trials, the discouraged hours, the fears and despair involved in works which have gained the admiration of the world, but which have taxed the utmost powers of their authors. You can read in a few minutes or a few hours a poem or a book with only pleasure and delight, but the days and months of weary plodding over details and dreary drudgery often required to produce it would stagger belief.

The greatest works in literature have been elaborated and elaborated, line by line, paragraph by paragraph, often rewritten a dozen times. The drudgery which literary writers have put into the productions which have stood the test of time is almost incredible. Lucretius worked nearly a lifetime on one poem. It completely absorbed his life. It is said that Bryant rewrote "Thanatopsis" a hundred times, and even then was not satisfied with it. John Foster would sometimes linger a week over a single sentence. He would hack, split, prune, pull up by the roots, or practice any other severity on whatever he wrote, till it gained his consent to exist. Chalmers was once asked what Foster was about in London. "Hard at it," he replied, "at the rate of a line a week." Dickens, one of the greatest writers of modern fiction, was so worn down by hard work that he looked as "haggard as a murderer." Even Lord Bacon, one of the greatest geniuses that ever lived, left large numbers of MSS. filled with "sudden thoughts set down for use." Hume toiled thirteen hours a day on his "History of England." Lord Eldon astonished the world with his great legal learning, but when he was a student too poor to buy books, he had actually borrowed and copied many hundreds of pages of large law books, such as Coke upon Littleton, thus saturating his mind with legal principles which afterward blossomed out into what the world called remarkable genius. Matthew Hale for years studied law sixteen hours a day. Speaking of Fox, some one declared that he wrote "drop by drop." Rousseau says of the labor involved in his smooth and lively style: "My manuscripts, blotted, scratched, interlined, and scarcely legible, attest the trouble they cost me. There is not one of them which I have not been obliged to transcribe four or five times before it went to press.... Some of my periods I have turned or returned in my head for five or six nights before they were fit to be put to paper."

It is said that Waller spent a whole summer over ten lines in one of his poems. Beethoven probably surpassed all other musicians in his painstaking fidelity and persistent application. There is scarcely a bar in his music that was not written and rewritten at least a dozen times. His favourite maxim was, "The barriers are not yet erected which can say to aspiring talent and industry 'thus far and no further.'" Gibbon wrote his autobiography nine times, and was in his study every morning, summer and winter, at six o'clock; and yet youth who waste their evenings wonder at the genius which can produce "The Decline and Fall of the Roman Empire," upon which Gibbon worked twenty years. Even Plato, one of the greatest writers that ever lived, wrote the first sentence in his "Republic" nine different ways before he was satisfied with it. Burke's famous "Letter to a Noble Lord," one of the finest things in the English language, was so completely blotted over with alterations when the proof was returned to the printing-office that the compositors refused to correct it as it was, and entirely reset it. Burke wrote the conclusion of his speech at the trial of Hastings sixteen times, and Butler wrote his famous "Analogy" twenty times. It took Virgil seven years to write his Georgics, and twelve years to write the Aeneid. He was so displeased with the latter that he attempted to rise from his deathbed to commit it to the flames.

* * *

When a man like Lord Cavanagh, without arms or legs, manages to put himself into Parliament, when a man like Francis Joseph Campbell, a blind man, becomes a distinguished mathematician, a musician, and a great philanthropist, we get a hint as to what it means to make the most possible out of ourselves and opportunities. Perhaps ninety-nine out of a hundred under such unfortunate circumstances would be content to remain helpless objects of charity for life. If it is your call to acquire money power instead of brain power, to acquire business power instead of professional power, double your talent just the same, no matter what it may be.

George Washington was the son of a widow, born under the roof of a Westmoreland farmer; almost from infancy his lot had been the lot of an orphan. No academy had welcomed him to its shade, no college crowned him with its honours; to read, to write, to cipher, these had been his degrees in knowledge. Shakespeare learned little more than reading and writing at school, but by self-culture he made himself the great master among literary men. Burns, too, enjoyed few advantages of education, and his youth was passed in almost abject poverty.

Julius Caesar, who has been unduly honoured for those great military achievements in which he appears as the scourge of his race, is far more deserving of respect for those wonderful Commentaries, in which his military exploits are recorded. He attained distinction by his writings on astronomy, grammar, history, and several other subjects. He was one of the most learned men and one of the greatest orators of his time. Yet his life was spent amid the turmoil of a camp or the fierce struggle of politics. If he found abundant time for study, who may not? Frederick the Great, too, was busy in camp the greater part of his life, yet whenever a leisure moment came, it was sure to be devoted to study. He wrote to a friend, "I become every day more covetous of my time, I render an account of it to myself, and I lose none of it but with great regret."

Columbus, while leading the life of a sailor, managed to become the most accomplished geographer and astronomer of his time.

*　　*　　*

The ancients said, "Know thyself;" the nineteenth century says, "Help thyself." Self-culture gives a second birth to the soul. A liberal education is a true regeneration. When a woman is once liberally educated, she will generally remain a woman, not shrink to a manikin, nor dwindle to a slave of circumstance. But if she is not properly educated, if she has merely been crammed and stuffed through college, if she has merely a broken-down memory from trying to hold crammed facts enough to pass the examination, she will continue to shrink and shrivel and dwindle, often below her original proportions, for she will lose both her confidence and self-respect, as her crammed facts, which never became a part of herself, evaporate from her distended memory. Many a girl has made her greatest effort in her graduating essay. But, alas! the beautiful flowers of rhetoric blossomed only to exhaust the parent stock, which blossoms no more forever.

*　　*　　*

True teaching will create a thirst for knowledge, and the desire to quench this thirst will lead to an eager student.

Every bit of education or culture is of great advantage in the struggle for existence. The microscope does not create anything new, but it reveals marvels. To educate the eye adds to its magnifying power until it sees beauty where before it saw only ugliness. It reveals a world we never suspected, and finds the greatest beauty even in the commonest things. The eye of an Agassiz could see worlds which the uneducated eye never dreamed of. The cultured hand can do a thousand things the uneducated hand cannot do. It becomes graceful, steady of nerve, strong, skilful, indeed it almost seems to think, so animated is it with intelligence. The cultured will can seize, grasp, and hold the possessor, with irresistible power and nerve, to almost superhuman effort. The educated touch can almost perform miracles. The educated taste can achieve wonders almost past belief.

"Culture comes from the constant choice of the best within our reach," says Bulwer. "Continue to cultivate the mind, to sharpen by exercise the genius, to attempt to delight or instruct your race; and, even supposing you fall short of every model you set before you, supposing your name moulder with your dust, still you will have passed life more nobly than the unlabourious herd. Grant that you win not that glorious accident, 'a name below,' how can you tell but that you may have fitted yourself for high destiny and employ, not in the world of men, but of spirits? The powers of the mind cannot be less immortal than the mere sense of identity; their acquisitions accompany us through the Eternal Progress, and we may obtain a lower or a higher grade hereafter, in proportion as we are more or less fitted by the exercise of our intellect to comprehend and execute the solemn agencies of God."

But be careful to avoid that over-intellectual culture which is purchased at the expense of moral vigour. An observant professor of one of our colleges has remarked that "the mind may be so rounded and polished by education, so well balanced, as not to be energetic in any one faculty. In others not thus trained, the sense of deficiency and of the sharp, jagged corners of their knowledge leads to efforts to fill up the chasms, rendering them at last far better educated than the polished, easy-going graduate who has just knowledge enough to prevent consciousness of ignorance. While all the faculties of the mind should be cultivated, it is yet desirable that it should have two or three rough-hewn features of massive strength."

In a gym you tug, you expand your chest, you push, pull, strike, run, jump, in order to develop your physical self; so you can develop your moral and intellectual nature only by continued effort.

All learning is self-teaching. It is upon the working of the pupil's own mind that her progress in knowledge depends. The great business of the master is to teach the pupil to teach herself.

* * *

The best education in the world is that got by struggling to obtain a living.—WENDELL PHILLIPS.

Who waits to have his task marked out,
Shall die and leave his errand unfulfilled.
LOWELL.

Let every eye negotiate for itself,
And trust no agent.
SHAKESPEARE.

CLEAR GRIT

I shall show the cinders of my spirits
Through the ashes of my chance.
SHAKESPEARE.

Let fortune empty her whole quiver on me,
I have a soul that, like an ample shield,
Can take in all, and verge enough for more.
DRYDEN.

Our greatest glory is not in never falling, but in rising every time we
fall.—GOLDSMITH.

Attempt the end and never stand to doubt;
Nothing's so hard but search will find it out.
HERRICK.

The barriers are not yet erected which shall say to aspiring talent, "Thus
far and no farther."—BEETHOVEN.

*　　*　　*

"Friends and comrades," said Pizarro, as he turned toward the south, after tracing with his sword upon the sand a line from east to west, "on that side are toil, hunger, nakedness, the drenching storm, desertion, and death; on this side, ease and pleasure. There lies Peru with its riches; here, Panama and its poverty. Choose, each man, what best becomes a brave Castilian. For my part, I go to the south." So saying, he crossed the line and was followed by thirteen Spaniards in armour. Thus, on the little island of Gallo in the Pacific, when his men were clamouring to return to Panama, did Pizarro and his few volunteers resolve to stake their lives upon the success of a desperate crusade against the powerful empire of the Incas. At the time they had not even a vessel to transport them to the country they wished to conquer. Is it necessary to add that all difficulties yielded at last to such resolute determination?

*　　*　　*

At a time when abolitionists were dangerously unpopular, a crowd of brawny Cape Cod fishermen had made such riotous demonstrations that all the speakers announced, except Stephen Foster and Lucy Stone, had fled from an open-air platform. "You had better run, Stephen," said she, "they are coming." "But who will take care of you?" asked Foster. "This gentleman will take care of me," she replied, calmly laying her hand within the arm of a burly rioter with a club, who had just sprung upon the platform. "Wh—what did you say?" stammered the astonished rowdy, as he looked at the little woman; "yes, I'll take care of you, and no one shall touch a hair of your head." With this he forced a way for her through the crowd, and, at her earnest request, placed her upon a stump and stood guard with his club while she delivered an address so effective that the audience offered no further violence, and even took up a collection of twenty dollars to repay Mr. Foster for the damage his clothes had received when the riot was at its height.

*　　*　　*

"When you get into a tight place and everything goes against you, till it seems as if you could not hold on a minute longer," said Harriet Beecher Stowe, "never give up then, for that's just the place and time that the tide'll turn."

Charles Sumner said, "Three things are necessary: first, backbone; second, backbone; third, backbone."

While digging among the ruins of Pompeii, which was buried by the dust and ashes from an eruption of Vesuvius, A. D. 79, the workmen found the skeleton of a Roman soldier in the sentry-box at one of the city's gates. He might have found safety under sheltering rocks close by; but, in the face of certain death, he had remained at his post, a mute witness to the thorough discipline, the ceaseless vigilance and fidelity which made the Roman legionaries masters of the known world. Bulwer, describing the flight of a party amid the dust, and ashes, and streams of boiling water, and huge hurtling fragments of scoria, and gusty winds, and lurid lightnings, continues: "The air was now still for a few minutes; the lamp from the gate streamed out far and clear; the fugitives hurried on. They gained the gate. They passed by the Roman sentry. The lightning flashed over his livid face and polished helmet, but his stern features were composed even in their awe! He remained erect and motionless at his post. That hour itself had not animated the machine of the ruthless majesty of Rome into the reasoning and self-acting man. There he stood amidst the crashing elements; he had not received the permission to desert his station and escape."

* * *

The world admires the woman who never flinches from unexpected difficulties, who calmly, patiently, and courageously grapples with her fate.

"Clear grit" always commands respect. It is that quality which achieves, and everybody admires achievement. In the strife of parties and principles, backbone without brains will carry against brains without backbone. "A politician weakly and amiably in the right is no match for a politician tenaciously and pugnaciously in the wrong." You cannot, by tying an opinion to a woman's tongue, make her the representative of that opinion; at the close of any battle for principles, her name will be found neither among the dead nor among the wounded, but among the missing.

* * *

The "London Times" was an insignificant sheet published by Mr. Walter and was steadily losing money. John Walter, Jr., then only twenty-seven years old, begged his father to give him full control of the paper. After many misgivings, the father finally consented. The young journalist began to remodel the establishment and to introduce new ideas everywhere. The paper had not attempted to mould public opinion, and had no individuality or character of its own. The audacious young editor boldly attacked every wrong, even the government, when he thought it corrupt. Thereupon the public customs, printing, and the government advertisements were withdrawn. The father was in utter dismay. The son he was sure would ruin the paper and himself. But no remonstrance could swerve him from his purpose, to give the world a great journal which should have weight, character, individuality, and independence. The public soon saw that a new power stood behind the "Times"; that its articles meant business; that new life and new blood and new ideas had been infused into the insignificant sheet; that a man with brains and push and tenacity of purpose stood at the helm,—a man who could make a way when he could not find one. Among other new features foreign dispatches were introduced, and they appeared in the "Times" several days before their appearance in the government organs. The "leading article" also was introduced to stay. But the aggressive editor antagonised the government, and his foreign dispatches were all stopped at the outpost, while those of the ministerial journalists were allowed to proceed. But nothing could daunt this resolute young spirit. At enormous expense he employed special couriers. Every obstacle put in his way, and all opposition from the government, only added to his determination to succeed. Enterprise, push, grit were behind the "Times," and nothing could stay its progress. Walter was the soul of the paper, and his personality pervaded every detail. In those days only three hundred copies of the "Times" could be struck off in an hour by the best presses, and Walter had duplicate and even triplicate types set. Then he set his brain to work, and finally the Walter Press, throwing off 17,000 copies, both sides printed, per hour, was the result. It was the 29th of November, 1814, that the first steam printed paper was given to the world. Walter's tenacity of purpose was remarkable. He shrank from no undertaking, and neglected no detail.

As a rule, pure grit, character, has the right of way. In the presence of women permeated with grit and sound in character, meanness and baseness slink out of sight. Mean women are uncomfortable, dishonesty trembles, hypocrisy is uncertain.

*　　*　　*

Lincoln, being asked by an anxious visitor what he would do after three or four years if the rebellion was not subdued, replied: "Oh, there is no alternative but to keep pegging away."

If impossibilities ever exist, popularly speaking, they ought to have been found somewhere between the birth and the death of Kitto, that deaf pauper and master of Oriental learning. But Kitto did not find them there. In the presence of his decision and imperial energy they melted away. Kitto begged his father to take him out of the poorhouse, even if he had to subsist like the Hottentots. He told him that he would sell his books and pawn his handkerchief, by which he thought he could raise about twelve shillings. He said he could live upon blackberries, nuts, and field turnips, and was willing to sleep on a hayrick. Here was real grit. What were impossibilities to such a resolute will?

Grit is a permanent, solid quality, which enters into the very structure, the very tissues of the constitution. A weak woman, a wavering, irresolute woman, may be "spunky" upon occasion, she may be "plucky" in an emergency; but pure "grit" is a part of the very character of strong women alone.

Demosthenes was a man who could rise to sublime heights of heroism, but his bravery was not his normal condition and depended upon his genius being aroused.

He had "pluck" and "spunk" on occasions, but Lincoln had pure "grit." When the illustrated papers everywhere were caricaturing him, when no epithet seemed too harsh to heap upon him, when his methods were criticised by his own party, and the generals in the war were denouncing his "foolish" confidence in Grant, and delegations were waiting upon him to ask for that general's removal, the great President sat with crossed legs, and was reminded of a story.

Lincoln and Grant both had that rare nerve which cares not for ridicule, is not swerved by public clamor, can bear abuse and hatred. There is a mighty force in truth and in the sublime conviction and supreme self-confidence behind it, in the knowledge that truth is mighty and the conviction and confidence that it will prevail.

The woman of grit carries in her very presence a power which controls and commands. She is spared the necessity of declaring herself, for her grit speaks in her every act. It does not come by fits and starts, it is a part of her very life. It inspires a sublime audacity and a heroic courage. Many of the failures of life are due to the want of grit or business nerve. It is unfortunate for a young woman to start out in business life with a weak, yielding disposition, with no resolution or backbone to mark her own course and stick to it, with no ability to say "No" with an emphasis, obliging this woman by investing in hopeless speculation, and rather than offend a friend, endorsing a questionable deal.

* * *

A little girl was asked how she learned to skate. "Oh, by getting up every time I fell down," she replied.

Whipple tells a story of Masséna which illustrates the masterful purpose that plucks victory out of the jaws of defeat. "After the defeat at Essling, the success of Napoleon's attempt to withdraw his beaten army depended on the character of Masséna, to whom the Emperor dispatched a messenger, telling him to keep his position for two hours longer at Aspern.

This order, couched in the form of a request, required almost an impossibility; but Napoleon knew the indomitable tenacity of the man to whom he gave it. The messenger found Masséna seated on a heap of rubbish, his eyes bloodshot, his frame weakened by his unparalleled exertions during a contest of forty hours, and his whole appearance indicating a physical state better befitting the hospital than the field. But that steadfast soul seemed altogether unaffected by bodily prostration; half dead as he was with fatigue, he rose painfully and said, 'Tell the Emperor that I will hold out for two hours.' And he kept his word."

"Never despair," says Burke, "but if you do, work on in despair."

It is victory after victory with the soldier, lesson after lesson with the scholar, blow after blow with the labourer, crop after crop with the farmer, picture after picture with the painter, and mile after mile with the traveler, that secures what all so much desire.

*　　*　　*

A promising Harvard student was stricken with paralysis of both legs. Physicians said there was no hope for him. The lad determined to continue his college studies. The examiners heard him at his bedside, and in four years he took his degree. He resolved to make a critical study of Dante, to do which he had to learn Italian and German. He persevered in spite of repeated attacks of illness and partial loss of sight. He was competing for the university prize. Think of the paralytic lad, helpless in bed, competing for a prize, fighting death inch by inch. What a lesson! Before his book was published or the prize awarded, the brave student died, but the book was successful. He meant that his life should not be a burden or a failure, and he was not only graduated from the best college in America, but competed successfully for the university prize, and made a valuable contribution to literature.

*　　*　　*

Orange Judd was a remarkable example of success through grit. He earned corn by working for farmers, carried it on his back to mill, brought back the meal to his room, cooked it himself, milked cows for his pint of milk per day, and lived on mush and milk for months together. He worked his way through Wesleyan University, and took a three years' post-graduate course at Yale.

President Chadbourne put grit in place of his lost lung, and worked thirty-five years after his funeral had been planned.

Lord Cavanagh put grit in the place of arms and legs, and went to Parliament in spite of his deformity.

Henry Fawcett put grit in place of eyesight, and became the greatest Postmaster-General England ever had.

Prescott also put grit in place of eyesight, and became one of America's greatest historians.

Thousands of women have also put grit in place of health, eyes, ears, hands, legs, and yet have achieved marvellous success. Indeed, most of the great things of the world have been accomplished by grit. You cannot keep a woman down who has this quality. She will make stepping-stones out of her stumbling-blocks, and lift herself to success.

*   *   *

See young Disraeli, sprung from a hated and persecuted race; without opportunity, pushing his way up through the middle classes, up through the upper classes, until he stands self-poised upon the topmost round of political and social power. Scoffed, ridiculed, rebuffed, hissed from the House of Commons, he simply says, "The time will come when you will hear me." The time did come, and the boy with no chance swayed the sceptre of England for a quarter of a century.

One of the most remarkable examples in history is Disraeli, forcing his leadership upon that very party whose prejudices were deepest against his race, and which had an utter contempt for self-made men and interlopers. Imagine England's surprise when she awoke to find this insignificant Hebrew actually Chancellor of the Exchequer. He was easily master of all the tortures supplied by the armoury of rhetoric; he could exhaust the resources of the bitterest invective; he could sting Gladstone out of his self-control; he was absolute master of himself and his situation. You can see that this young man intends to make his way in the world. A determined audacity is in his very face. He is a gay fop. Handsome, with the hated Hebrew blood in his veins, after three defeats in parliamentary elections he was not the least daunted, for he knew his day would come, as it did. Lord Melbourne, the great Prime Minister, when this gay young fop was introduced to him, asked him what he wished to be. "Prime Minister of England," was his audacious reply.

*　*　*

William H. Seward was given a thousand dollars by his father to go to college with; this was all he was to have. The son returned at the end of the freshman year with extravagant habits and no money. His father refused to give him more, and told him he could not stay at home. When the youth found the props all taken out from under him, and that he must now sink or swim, he left home moneyless, returned to college, graduated at the head of his class, studied law, was elected Governor of New York, and became Lincoln's great Secretary of State during the Civil War.

Louisa M. Alcott wrote the conclusion to "An Old-Fashioned Girl" with her left hand in a sling, one foot up, head aching, and no voice. She proudly writes in her diary, "Twenty years ago I resolved to make the family independent if I could. At forty, that is done. Debts all paid, even the outlawed ones, and we have enough to be comfortable. It has cost me my health, perhaps." She earned two hundred thousand dollars by her pen.

Mrs. Frank Leslie often refers to the time she lived in her carpetless attic while striving to pay her deceased husband's obligations. She has fought her way successfully through nine lawsuits, and paid the entire debt. She managed her ten publications entirely herself, signed all checks and money-orders, made all contracts, looked over all proofs, and ran a booming business.

*　*　*

The race is not always to the swift, the battle is not always to the strong. Horses are sometimes weighted or hampered in the race, and this is taken into account in the result. So in the race of life the distance alone does not determine the prize. We must take into consideration the hindrances, the weights we have carried, the disadvantages of education, of breeding, of training, of surroundings, of circumstances. How many young women are weighted down with debt, with poverty, with the supporting of invalid parents or brothers and sisters, or children? How many are fettered with ignorance, hampered by inhospitable surroundings, with the opposition of parents who do not understand them? How many are delayed in their course because nobody believes in them, because nobody encourages them, because they get no sympathy and are forever tortured for not doing that against which every fibre of their being protests, and every drop of their blood rebels? How many have to feel their way to the goal, through the blindness of ignorance and lack of experience? How many go bungling along from the lack of early discipline and drill in the vocation they have

94

chosen? How many have to hobble along on crutches because they were never taught to help themselves, but to lean upon a father's wealth or a mother's indulgence? How many are weakened for the journey of life by self-indulgence, by dissipation, by "life-sappers;" how many are crippled by disease, by a weak constitution, by impaired eyesight or hearing?

When the prizes of life shall be awarded by the Supreme Judge, who knows our weaknesses and frailties, the distance we have run, the weights we have carried, the handicaps, will all be taken into account. Not the distance we have run, but the obstacles we have overcome, the disadvantages under which we have made the race, will decide the prizes. The poor wretch who has plodded along against unknown temptations, the poor woman who has buried her sorrows in her silent heart and sewed her weary way through life, those who have suffered abuse in silence, and who have been unrecognised or despised by their fellow-runners, will often receive the greater prize.

*　　*　　*

"The wise and active conquer difficulties,
By daring to attempt them: sloth and folly
Shiver and sink at sight of toil and hazard,
And make the impossibility they fear."

Tumble me down, and I will sit
Upon my ruins, smiling yet:
Tear me to tatters, yet I'll be
Patient in my necessity:
Laugh at my scraps of clothes, and shun
Me as a fear'd infection:
Yet scare-crow like I'll walk, as one
Neglecting thy derision.
ROBERT HERRICK.

WEALTH IN ECONOMY

Economy is the parent of integrity, of liberty and ease, and the beauteous sister of temperance, of cheerfulness and health.—DR. JOHNSON.

Can anything be so elegant as to have few wants and to serve them one's self?

As much wisdom can be expended on a private economy as on an empire.—EMERSON.

Riches amassed in haste will diminish; but those collected by hand and little by little will multiply.—GOETHE.

No gain is so certain as that which proceeds from the economical use of what you have.—LATIN PROVERB.

Beware of little extravagances: a small leak will sink a big ship.— FRANKLIN.

Not for to hide it in a hedge,
Nor for a train attendant,
But for the glorious privilege
Of being independent.
BURNS.

* * *

Emerson relates the following anecdote: "An opulent merchant in

Boston was called on by a friend in behalf of a charity. At that time he was admonishing his clerk for using whole wafers instead of halves; his friend thought the circumstance unpropitious; but to his surprise, on listening to the appeal, the merchant subscribed five hundred dollars. The applicant expressed his astonishment that any person who was so particular about half a wafer should present five hundred dollars to a charity; but the merchant said, "It is by saving half wafers, and attending to such little things, that I have now something to give."

*   *   *

If you begin at age twenty to save 15% of your income, and you only earn $35,000 per year until you were 65 years old, you would have saved $5.5 million! If you continued working until you were 75 years old, just another 10 years, your savings would compound to $15 million. Even a saving of one dollar a week from the date of one's majority would give him one thousand dollars for each of the last ten of the allotted years of life. "What maintains one vice would bring up two children."

Such rigid economy, such high courage, enables one to surprise the world with gifts even if she is poor. In fact, the poor and the middle classes give most in the aggregate to charities and hospitals and to the poor. Only frugality enables them to outdo the rich on their own ground.

But miserliness or avariciousness is a different thing from economy. The miserly is the miserable woman, who hoards money from a love of it. A miser who spends a cent upon herself where another would spend a quarter does it from parsimony, which is a subordinate characteristic of avarice.

A writer on political economy tells of the mishaps resulting from a broken latch on a farmyard gate. Every one going through would shut the gate, but as the latch would not hold it, it would swing open with every breeze. One day a pig ran out into the woods. Every one on the farm went to help get him back. A gardener jumped over a ditch to stop the pig, and sprained his ankle so badly as to be confined to his bed for two weeks. When the cook returned, she found that her linen, left to dry at the fire, was all badly scorched. The dairymaid in her excitement left the cows untied, and one of them broke the leg of a colt. The gardener lost several hours of valuable time. Yet a new latch would not have cost five cents.

Guy, the London bookseller, and afterward the founder of the great hospital, was a great miser, living in the back part of his shop, eating upon an old bench, and using his counter for a table, with a newspaper for a cloth. He did not marry. One day he was visited by "Vulture" Hopkins, another well-known miser. "What is your business?" asked Guy, lighting a candle. "To discuss your methods of saving money," was the reply, alluding to the niggardly economy for which Guy was famous. On learning Hopkins's business he blew out the light, saying, "We can do that in the dark." "Sir, you are my master in the art," said the "Vulture;" "I need ask no further. I see where your secret lies."

Yet that kind of economy which verges on the niggardly is better than the extravagance that laughs at it. Either, when carried to excess, is not only apt to cause misery, but to ruin the character.

"Wealth, a monster gorged
'Mid starving populations."

*　　*　　*

But nowhere and at no period were these contrasts more startling than in Imperial Rome. There a whole population might be trembling lest they should be starved by the delay of an Alexandrian corn-ship, while the upper classes were squandering fortunes at a single banquet, drinking out of myrrhine and jewelled vases worth hundreds of pounds, and feasting on the brains of peacocks and the tongues of nightingales. As a consequence, disease was rife, men were short-lived. At this time the dress of Roman ladies displayed an unheard-of splendour. The elder Pliny tells us that he himself saw Lollia Paulina dressed for a betrothal feast in a robe entirely covered with pearls and emeralds, which had cost 40,000,000 sesterces, and which was known to be less costly than some of her other dresses. Gluttony, caprice, extravagance, ostentation, impurity, rioted in the heart of a society which knew of no other means by which to break the monotony of its weariness or alleviate the anguish of its despair.

A woman once bought an old door-plate with "Thompson" on it because she thought it might come in handy some time. The habit of buying what you don't need because it is cheap encourages extravagance. "Many have been ruined by buying good pennyworths."

"Where there is no prudence," said Dr. Johnson, "there is no virtue."

Many a young woman seems to think that when she sees her name on a business card she is on the highway to fortune, and she begins to live on a scale as though there was no possible chance of failure; as though she were already beyond the danger point. Unfortunately parliament can pass no law that will remedy the vice of living beyond one's means.

"However easy it may be to make money," said Barnum, "it is the most difficult thing in the world to keep it."

*   *   *

Very few women know how to use money properly. They can earn it, lavish it, hoard it, waste it, but to deal with it wisely, as a means to an end, is an education difficult of acquirement.

To do your best you must own every bit of yourself. If you are in debt, part of you belongs to your creditors.

The "loose change" which many young women throw away carelessly, or worse, would often form the basis of a fortune and independence. The woman without a penny is practically helpless, from a business point of view, except so far as she can immediately utilise her powers of body and mind. Besides, when a man or woman is driven to the wall, the chance of goodness surviving self-respect and the loss of public esteem is frightfully diminished.

"Money goes as it comes."

Live between extravagance and meanness. Don't save money and starve your mind. The very secret and essence of thrift consists in getting things into higher values. Spend upward, that is, for the higher faculties. Spend for the mind rather than for the body, for culture rather than for amusement.

Liberal, not lavish, is Nature's hand. Even God, it is said, cannot afford to be extravagant. When He increased the loaves and fishes, He commanded to gather up the fragments, that nothing be lost.

*   *   *

"Nature uses a grinding economy," says Emerson, working up all that is wasted today into tomorrow's creation; not a superfluous grain of sand for all the ostentation she makes of expense and public works. She flung us out in her plenty, but we cannot shed a hair or a paring of a nail but instantly she snatches at the shred and appropriates it to her general stock." Last summer's flowers and foliage decayed in autumn only to enrich the earth this year for other forms of beauty. Nature will not even wait for our friends to see us, unless we die at home. The moment the breath has left the body she begins to take us to pieces, that the parts may be used again for other creations.

It is by the mysterious power of economy, it has been said, that the loaf is multiplied, that using does not waste, that little becomes much, that scattered fragments grow to unity, and that out of nothing or next to nothing comes the miracle of something. It is not merely saving, still less, parsimony. It is foresight and arrangement, insight and combination, causing inert things to labour, useless things to serve our necessities, perishing things to renew their vigour, and all things to exert themselves for human comfort.

*　　*　　*

Washington examined the minutest expenditures of his family, even when President of the United States. He understood that without economy none can be rich, and with it none need be poor.

"I make a point of paying my own bills," said Wellington.

John Jacob Astor said that the first thousand dollars cost him more effort than all of his millions. Girls who are careless with their dimes and quarters, just because they have so few, never get this first thousand, and without it no fortune is possible.

To find out uses for the persons or things which are now wasted in life is to be the glorious work of the women of the next generation, and that which will contribute most to their enrichment.

Economising "in spots" or by freaks is no economy at all. It must be done by management.

Learn early in life to say "I can't afford it." It is an indication of power and courage and manliness.

Dr. Franklin said, "It is not our own eyes, but other people's, that ruin us."

"Fashion wears out more apparel than the [wo]man," says Shakespeare.

If a man owes you a dollar, he is almost sure to owe you a grudge, too. If you owe another money, you will be apt to regard her with uncharitable eyes. Why not economise before getting into debt instead of pinching afterwards?

Communities which live wholly from hand to mouth never make much progress in the useful arts. Savings mean power. Comfort and independence abide with those who can postpone their desires.

"Hunger, rags, cold, hard work, contempt, suspicion, unjust reproach, are disagreeable," says Horace Greeley, "but debt is infinitely worse than them all."

Many a ruined man dates his downfall from the day when he began borrowing money.

"We are ruined," says Colton, "not by what we really want, but by what we think we do. Therefore never go abroad in search of your wants; if they be real wants, they will come home in search of you; for he that buys what he does not want will soon want what he cannot buy."

The honourable course is to give every woman her due. It is better to starve than not to do this. It is better to do a small business on a cash basis than a large one on credit. "Owe no man anything", wrote St. Paul. It is a good motto to place in every purse, in every counting-room, in every church, in every home.

* * *

Economy is of itself a great revenue.—CICERO.

I can get no remedy against this consumption of the purse; borrowing only lingers and lingers it out; but the disease is incurable.— SHAKESPEARE.

Whatever be your talents, whatever be your prospects, never speculate away on the chance of a palace that which you may need as a provision against the workhouse.—BULWER

RICH WITHOUT MONEY

Let others plead for pensions; I can be rich without money, by endeavouring to be superior to everything poor. I would have my services to my country unstained by any interested motive.—LORD COLLINGWOOD.

Pennilessness is not poverty, and ownership is not possession; to be without is not always to lack, and to reach is not to attain; sunlight is for all eyes that look up, and colour for those who choose.—HELEN HUNT.

To be content with what we possess is the greatest and most secure of riches.—CICERO.

There is no riches above a sound body and no joy above the joy of the heart.—ECCLESIASTES.

A great heart in a little house is of all things here below that which has ever touched me most.—LACORDAIRE.

*   *   *

Many a woman is rich without money. Thousands of women with nothing in their pockets, and thousands without even a pocket, are rich.

A woman born with a good, sound constitution, a good stomach, a good heart and good limbs, and a pretty good headpiece, is rich.

Good bones are better than gold, tough muscles than silver, and nerves that carry energy to every function are better than houses and land.

* * *

"Heart-life, soul-life, hope, joy, and love, are true riches," said Beecher. "Why should I scramble and struggle to get possession of a little portion of this earth? This is my world now; why should I envy others its mere legal possession? It belongs to those who can see it, enjoy it. I need not envy the so-called owners of estates in Boston and New York. They are merely taking care of my property and keeping it in excellent condition for me. For a few pennies for railroad fare whenever I wish I can see and possess the best of it all. It has cost me no effort, it gives me no care; yet the green grass, the shrubbery, and the statues on the lawns, the finer sculptures and the paintings within, are always ready for me whenever I feel a desire to look upon them. I do not wish to carry them home with me, for I could not give them half the care they now receive; besides, it would take too much of my valuable time, and I should be worrying continually lest they be spoiled or stolen. I have much of the wealth of the world now. It is all prepared for me without any pains on my part. All around me are working hard to get things that will please me, and competing to see who can give them the cheapest. The little I pay for the use of libraries, railroads, galleries, parks, is less than it would cost to care for the least of all I use. Life and landscape are mine, the stars and flowers, the sea and air, the birds and trees. What more do I want? All the ages have been working for me; all mankind are my servants. I am only required to feed and clothe myself, an easy task in this land of opportunity."

* * *

A millionaire pays thousands of pounds for a gallery of paintings, and some poor boy or girl comes in, with open mind and poetic fancy, and carries away a treasure of beauty which the owner never saw. A collector bought at public auction in London, an autograph of Shakespeare; but for nothing a school girl can read and absorb the riches of "Hamlet."

Why should I waste my abilities pursuing this will-o'-the-wisp "Enough," which is ever a little more than one has, and which none of the panting millions ever yet overtook in his mad chase? Is there no desirable thing left in this world but gold, luxury, and ease?

Want is a growing giant whom the coat of Have was never large enough to cover. "A [wo]man may as soon fill a chest with grace, or a vessel with virtue," says Phillips Brooks, "as a heart with wealth."

Shall we seek happiness through the sense of taste or of touch? Shall we idolise our stomachs and our backs? Have we no higher missions, no nobler destinies? Shall we "disgrace the fair day by a pusillanimous preference of our bread to our freedom"?

In the three great "Banquets" of Plato, Xenophon, and Plutarch the food is not even mentioned.

* * *

What does your money say to you: what message does it bring to you? Does it say to you, "Eat, drink, and be merry, for tomorrow we die"? Does it bring a message of comfort, of education, of culture, of travel, of books, of an opportunity to help your fellow-man, or is the message "More land, more thousands and millions"? What message does it bring you? Clothes for the naked, bread for the starving, schools for the ignorant, hospitals for the sick, asylums for the orphans, or of more for yourself and none for others? Is it a message of generosity or of meanness, breadth or narrowness? Does it speak to you of character? Does it mean a broader womanhood, a larger aim, a nobler ambition, or does it cry "More, more, more"?

Are you an animal loaded with ingots, or a woman filled with a purpose? She is rich whose mind is rich, whose thought enriches the intellect of the world. It is a sad sight to see a soul which thirsts not for truth or beauty or the good.

A sailor on a sinking vessel in the Caribbean Sea eagerly filled his pockets with Spanish dollars from a barrel on board while his companions, about to leave in the only boat, begged him to seek safety with them. But he could not leave the bright metal which he had so longed for and idolised, and was prevented from reaching shore by his very riches, when the vessel went down.

* * *

"Who is the richest of men," asked Socrates? "He who is content with the least, for contentment is nature's riches."

In More's "Utopia" gold was despised. Criminals were forced to wear heavy chains of it, and to have rings of it in their ears; it was put to the vilest uses to keep up the scorn of it. Bad characters were compelled to wear gold head-bands. Diamonds and pearls were used to decorate infants, so that the youth would discard and despise them.

"Ah, if the rich were as rich as the poor fancy riches!" exclaims Emerson.

Many a rich man has died in the poorhouse.

In excavating Pompeii a skeleton was found with the fingers clenched round a quantity of gold. A man of business in the town of Hull, England, when dying, pulled a bag of money from under his pillow, which he held between his clenched fingers with a grasp so firm as scarcely to relax under the agonies of death.

*   *   *

Oh! blind and wanting wit to choose,
Who house the chaff and burn the grain;
Who hug the wealth ye cannot use,
And lack the riches all may gain.
WILLIAM WATSON.

*   *   *

Poverty is the want of much, avarice the want of everything.

A poor woman was met by a stranger while scoffing at the wealthy for not enjoying themselves. The stranger gave her a purse, in which she was always to find a dollar. As fast as she took one out another was to drop in, but she was not to begin to spend her fortune until she had thrown away the purse. She takes dollar after dollar out, but continually procrastinates and puts off the hour of enjoyment until she has got "a little more," and dies at last counting her millions.

A beggar was once met by Fortune, who promised to fill his wallet with gold, as much as he might please, on condition that whatever touched the ground should turn at once to dust. The beggar opens his wallet, asks for more and yet more, until the bag bursts. The gold falls to the ground, and all is lost.

When the steamer Central America was about to sink, the stewardess, having collected all the gold she could from the staterooms, and tied it in her apron, jumped for the last boat leaving the steamer. She missed her aim and fell into the water, the gold carrying her down head first.

Some women are rich in health, in constant cheerfulness, in a mercurial temperament which floats them over troubles and trials enough to sink a shipload of ordinary women. Others are rich in disposition, family, and friends. There are some women so amiable that everybody loves them; some so cheerful that they carry an atmosphere of jollity about them. Some are rich in integrity and character.

* * *

One of the first great lessons of life is to learn the true estimate of values. As the girl starts out in her career, all sorts of wares will be imposed upon her, and all kinds of temptations will be used to induce her to buy. Her success will depend very largely upon her ability to estimate properly, not the apparent but the real value of everything presented to her. A thousand different schemes will be thrust into her face with their claims for superiority. Every occupation and vocation will present its charms in turn, and offer its inducements. The youth who would succeed must not allow herself to be deceived by appearances, but must place the emphasis of life where it belongs.

No man, it is said, can read the works of John Ruskin without learning that his sources of pleasure are well-nigh infinite. There is not a flower, nor a cloud, nor a tree, nor a mountain, nor a star; not a bird that fans the air, nor a creature that walks the earth; not a glimpse of sea or sky or meadow-greenery; not a work of worthy art in the domains of painting, sculpture, poetry, and architecture; not a thought of God as the Great Spirit presiding over and informing all things, that is not to him a source of the sweetest pleasure. The whole world of matter and of spirit and the long record of human art are open to him as the never-failing fountains of his delight. In these pure realms he seeks his daily food and has his daily life.

There is now and then a woman who sees beauty and true riches everywhere, and "worships the splendour of God which she sees bursting through each chink and cranny."

* * *

We all live on far lower levels than we need to do. We linger in the misty and oppressive valleys, when we might be climbing the sunlit hills. Emerson says, "We have come into a world which is a living poem. Everything is as I am." Nature provides for us a perpetual festival; she is bright to the bright, comforting to those who will accept comfort. We cannot conceive how a

106

universe could possibly be created which could devise more efficient methods or greater opportunities for the delight, the happiness, and the real wealth of human beings than the one we live in.

The human body is packed full of marvellous devices, of wonderful contrivances, of infinite possibilities for the happiness and riches of the individual. No physiologist nor scientist has ever yet been able to point out a single improvement, even in the minutest detail, in the structure of the human body. No inventor has ever yet been able to suggest an improvement in this human mechanism. No chemist has ever been able to suggest a superior combination in any one of the elements which make up the human structure. One of the first things to do in life is to learn the natural wealth of our surroundings, instead of bemoaning our lot, for, no matter where we are placed, there is infinitely more about us than we can ever understand, than we can ever exhaust the meaning of.

*　　*　　*

Raphael was rich without money. All doors opened to him, and he was more than welcome everywhere. His sweet spirit radiated sunshine wherever he went.

Mozart, the great composer of the "Requiem," left barely enough money to bury him, but he has made the world richer.

A rich mind and noble spirit will cast a radiance of beauty over the humblest home, which the upholsterer and decorator can never approach. Who would not prefer to be a millionaire of character, of contentment, rather than possess nothing but the vulgar coins of a Croesus? Whoever uplifts civilisation is rich though she dies penniless, and future generations will erect her monument.

An Asiatic traveler tells us that one day he found the bodies of two men laid upon the desert sand beside the carcass of a camel. They had evidently died from thirst, and yet around the waist of each was a large store of jewels of different kinds, which they had doubtless been crossing the desert to sell in the markets of Persia.

The woman who has no money is poor, but one who has nothing but money is poorer than she. She only is rich who can enjoy without owning; she who is covetous is poor though she have millions. There are riches of intellect, and no woman with an intellectual taste can be called poor. She who has so little knowledge of human nature as to seek happiness by changing anything but her own disposition will waste her life in fruitless efforts, and multiply the griefs which she purposes to remove. She is rich as well as brave who can face poverty and misfortune with cheerfulness and courage.

*   *   *

We can so educate the will power that it will focus the thoughts upon the bright side of things, and upon objects which elevate the soul, thus forming a habit of happiness and goodness which will make us rich. The habit of making the best of everything and of always looking on the bright side of everything is a fortune in itself.

She is rich who values a good name above gold. Among the ancient Greeks and Romans honour was more sought after than wealth. Rome was imperial Rome no more when the imperial purple became an article of traffic.

Diogenes was captured by pirates and sold as a slave. His purchaser released him, and gave him charge of his household and of the education of his children. He despised wealth and affectation, and lived in a tub. "Do you want anything?" asked Alexander the Great, forcibly impressed by the abounding cheerfulness of the philosopher under such circumstances. "Yes," replied Diogenes, "I want you to stand out of my sunshine and not to take from me what you cannot give me." "Were I not Alexander," exclaimed the great conqueror, "I would be Diogenes."

"I don't want such things," said Epictetus to the rich Roman orator who was making light of his contempt for money-wealth; "and besides," said the stoic, "you are poorer than I am, after all. You have silver vessels, but earthenware reasons, principles, appetites. My mind to me a kingdom is, and it furnishes me with abundant and happy occupation in lieu of your restless idleness. All your possessions seem small to you; mine seem great to me. Your desire is insatiate, mine is satisfied."

*   *   *

A bankrupt merchant, returning home one night, said to his noble wife, "My dear, I am ruined; everything we have is in the hands of the sheriff."

After a few moments of silence the wife looked into his face and asked, "Will the sheriff sell you?"

"Oh, no."

"Will the sheriff sell me?"

"Oh, no."

"Then do not say we have lost everything. All that is most valuable remains to us,—manhood, womanhood, childhood. We have lost but the results of our skill and industry. We can make another fortune if our hearts and hands are left us."

* * *

What power can poverty have over a home where loving hearts are beating with a consciousness of untold riches of head and heart?

"Character before wealth," was the motto of Amos Lawrence, who had inscribed on his pocket-book, "What shall it profit a [wo]man, if [s]he shall gain the whole world and lose [her] own soul?"

If you make a fortune let every dollar of it be clean. You do not want to see in it drunkards reel, orphans weep, widows moan. Your riches must not make others poorer and more wretched.

Don't start out in life with a false standard; a truly great woman makes official position and money and houses and estates look so tawdry, so mean and poor, that we feel like sinking out of sight with our cheap laurels and gold. Millions look trifling beside character.

A friend of Professor Agassiz, an eminent practical man, once expressed his wonder that a man of such abilities should remain contented with such a moderate income as he received. "I have enough," was Agassiz's reply. "I have no time to waste in making money. Life is not sufficiently long to enable a man to get rich and do his duty to his fellow-men at the same time."

* * *

How were the thousands of business men who lost every dollar they had in the Chicago fire enabled to go into business at once, some into wholesale business, without money? Their record was their bank account. The commercial agencies said they were square men; that they had always paid one hundred cents on a dollar; that they had paid promptly, and that they were industrious and dealt honourably with all men. This record was as good as a bank account. They drew on their character. Character was the coin which enabled penniless men to buy thousands of dollars' worth of goods. Their integrity did not burn up with their stores. The best part of them was beyond the reach of fire and could not be burned.

"There are treasures laid up in the heart—treasures of charity, piety, temperance, and soberness. These treasures a [wo]man takes with [her] beyond death when [s]he leaves this world." (Buddhist Scriptures.)

Is it any wonder that our children start out with wrong ideals of life, with wrong ideas of what constitutes success? The child is "urged to get on," to "rise in the world," to "make money." The girl is constantly told that nothing succeeds like success. False standards are everywhere set up for her, and then the girl is blamed if she makes a failure.

It is all very well to urge girls on to success, but the great mass of mankind can never reach or even approximate the goal constantly preached to them, nor can we all be rich. One of the great lessons to teach in this century of sharp competition and the survival of the fittest is how to be rich without money, and to learn how to do without success, according to the popular standard (financial wealth).

Gold cannot make the miser rich, nor can the want of it make the beggar poor.

*   *   *

In the poem, "The Changed Cross," a weary woman is represented as dreaming that she was led to a place where many crosses lay, crosses of divers shapes and sizes. The most beautiful one was set in jewels of gold. It was so tiny and exquisite that she changed her own plain cross for it, thinking she was fortunate in finding one so much lighter and lovelier. But soon her back began to ache under the glittering burden, and she changed it for another cross very beautiful and entwined with flowers. But she soon found that underneath the flowers were piercing thorns which tore her flesh. At last she came to a very plain cross without jewels, without carving, and with only the word, "Love," inscribed upon it. She took this one up and it proved the easiest and best of all. She was amazed, however, to find that it was her old cross which she had discarded. It is easy to see the jewels and the flowers in other people's crosses, but the thorns and heavy weight are known only to the bearers. How easy other people's burdens seem to us compared with our own. We do not appreciate the secret burdens which almost crush the heart, nor the years of weary waiting for delayed success—the aching hearts longing for sympathy, the hidden poverty, the suppressed emotion in other lives.

The object for which we strive tells the story of our lives. Men and women should be judged by the happiness they create in those around them. Noble deeds always enrich, but millions of mere money may impoverish. Character is perpetual wealth, and by the side of her who possesses it the millionaire who has it not seems a pauper. Compared with it, what are houses and lands, stocks and bonds? "It is better that great souls should live in small habitations than that abject slaves should burrow in great houses." Plain living, rich thought, and grand effort are real riches.

Invest in yourself, and you will never be poor. Floods cannot carry your wealth away, fire cannot burn it, rust cannot consume it.

*   *   *

Howe'er it be, it seems to me,
'T is only noble to be good.
Kind hearts are more than coronets,
And simple faith than Norman blood.
TENNYSON.

He is richest who is content with the least, for content is the wealth of nature.—SOCRATES.

My crown is in my heart, not on my head,
Nor decked with diamonds and Indian stones,
Nor to be seen: my crown is called content;
A crown it is, that seldom kings enjoy.
SHAKESPEAKE.

OPPORTUNITIES WHERE YOU ARE

To each man's life there comes a time supreme;
One day, one night, one morning, or one noon,
One freighted hour, one moment opportune,
One rift through which sublime fulfillments gleam,
One space when fate goes tiding with the stream,
One Once, in balance 'twixt Too Late, Too Soon,
And ready for the passing instant's boon
To tip in favour the uncertain beam.
Ah, happy he who, knowing how to wait,
Knows also how to watch and work and stand
On Life's broad deck alert, and at the prow
To seize the passing moment, big with fate,
From opportunity's extended hand,
When the great clock of destiny strikes Now!
MARY A. TOWNSEND.

A thousand years a poor man watched
Before the gate of Paradise:
But while one little nap he snatched,
It opened and shut. Ah! was he wise?
W. B. ALGER.

Our grand business is, not to see what lies dimly at a distance, but to do
what lies clearly at hand.—CARLYLE.

A [wo]man's best things are nearest [her],
Lie close about his feet.
R. M. MILNES.

The secret of success in life is for a [wo]man to be ready for [her] opportunity when it comes.—DISRAELI.

*   *   *

No chance, no opportunities, in a land where many poor girls become rich women, and where those born in the lowest stations attain the highest positions? The world is all gates, all opportunities to her who will use them. But, like Bunyan's Pilgrim in the dungeon of Giant Despair's castle, who had the key of deliverance all the time with him but had forgotten it, we fail to rely wholly upon the ability to advance all that is good for us which has been given to the weakest as well as the strongest. We depend too much upon outside assistance.

A Baltimore lady lost a valuable diamond bracelet at a ball, and supposed that it was stolen from the pocket of her cloak. Years afterward she washed the steps of the Peabody Institute, pondering how to get money to buy food. She cut up an old, worn-out, ragged cloak to make a hood, when lo! in the lining of the cloak she discovered the diamond bracelet. During all her poverty she was worth $3500, but did not know it.

Many of us who think we are poor are rich in opportunities, if we could only see them, in possibilities all about us, in faculties worth more than diamond bracelets. It is a sorry day for a young woman who cannot see any opportunities where she is, but thinks she can do better somewhere else.

The richest gold and silver mine in Nevada was sold for $42 by the owner to get money to pay his passage to other mines, where he thought he could get rich. Professor Agassiz told the Harvard students of a farmer who owned a farm of hundreds of acres of unprofitable woods and rocks, and concluded to sell out and get into a more profitable business. He decided to go into the coal-oil business; he studied coal measures and coal-oil deposits, and experimented for a long time. He sold his farm for $200, and engaged in his new business two hundred miles away. Only a short time after the man who bought his farm discovered upon it a great flood of coal-oil, which the farmer had previously ignorantly tried to drain off.

*   *   *

Hundreds of years ago there lived near the shore of the river Indus a Persian by the name of Ali Hafed. He lived in a cottage on the river bank, from which he could get a grand view of the beautiful country stretching away to the sea. He had a wife and children, an extensive farm, fields of grain, gardens of flowers, orchards of fruit, and miles of forest. He had a plenty of money and everything that heart could wish. He was contented and happy.

One evening a priest of Buddha visited him, and, sitting before the fire, explained to him how the world was made, and how the first beams of sunlight condensed on the earth's surface into diamonds. The old priest told that a drop of sunlight the size of his thumb was worth more than large mines of copper, silver, or gold; that with one of them he could buy many farms like his; that with a handful he could buy a province, and with a mine of diamonds he could purchase a kingdom. Ali Hafed listened, and was no longer a rich man. He had been touched with discontent, and with that all wealth vanishes.

Early the next morning he woke the priest who had been the cause of his unhappiness, and anxiously asked him where he could find a mine of diamonds. "What do you want of diamonds?" asked the astonished priest.

"I want to be rich and place my children on thrones."

"All you have to do is to go and search until you find them," said the priest.

"But where shall I go?" asked the poor farmer.

"Go anywhere, north, south, east, or west."

"How shall I know when I have found the place?"

"When you find a river running over white sands between high mountain ranges, in those white sands you will find diamonds," answered the priest.

The discontented man sold the farm for what he could get, left his family with a neighbour, took the money he had at interest, and went to search for the coveted treasure. Over the mountains of Arabia, through Palestine and Egypt, he wandered for years, but found no diamonds. When his money was all gone and starvation stared him in the face, ashamed of his folly and of his rags, poor Ali Hafed threw himself into the tide and was drowned.

The man who bought his farm was a contented man, who made the most of his surroundings, and did not believe in going away from home to hunt for diamonds or success. While his camel was drinking in the garden one day, he noticed a flash of light from the white sands of the brook. He picked up a pebble, and pleased with its brilliant hues took it into the house, put it on the shelf near the fireplace, and forgot all about it.

The old priest of Buddha who had filled Ali Hafed with the fatal discontent called one day upon the new owner of the farm. He had no sooner entered the room than his eye caught that flash of light from the stone. "Here's a diamond! here's a diamond!" the old priest shouted in great excitement. "Has Ali Hafed returned?" said the priest.

"No," said the farmer, "nor is that a diamond. That is but a stone." They went into the garden and stirred up the white sand with their fingers, and behold, other diamonds more beautiful than the first gleamed out of it. So the famous diamond beds of Golconda were discovered. Had Ali Hafed been content to remain at home, had he dug in his own garden, instead of going abroad in search for wealth, and reaping poverty, hardships, starvation, and death, he would have been one of the richest men in the world, for the entire farm abounded in the richest of gems.

*   *   *

You have your own special place and work. Find it, fill it. Scarcely a boy or girl will read these lines but has much better opportunity to win success than Garfield, Wilson, Franklin, Lincoln, Harriet Beecher Stowe, Frances Willard, and thousands of others. But to succeed you must be prepared to seize and improve the opportunity when it comes. Remember that four things come not back: the spoken word, the sped arrow, the past life, and the neglected opportunity.

It is one of the paradoxes of civilisation that the more opportunities are utilised, the more new ones are thereby created. New openings are as easy to fill as ever to those who do their best; although it is not so easy as formerly to obtain distinction in the old lines, because the standard has advanced so much and competition has so greatly increased. "The world is no longer clay," said Emerson, "but rather iron in the hands of its workers, and men have got to hammer out a place for themselves by steady and rugged blows."

Thousands of women have made fortunes out of trifles which others pass by. As the bee gets honey from the same flower from which the spider gets poison, so some women will get a fortune out of the commonest and simplest things, as scraps of leather, cotton waste, soap, iron filings, from which others get only poverty and failure. There is scarcely a thing which contributes to the welfare and comfort of humanity, not an article of household furniture, a kitchen utensil, an article of clothing or of food, that is not capable of an improvement in which there may be a fortune.

*   *   *

Opportunities? They are all around us. Edison found them in a baggage car. Forces of nature plead to be used, as lightning for ages tried to attract human attention to the great force of electricity, which would do much of the drudgery and leave humans to develop the God-given powers within them. There is power lying latent everywhere waiting for the observant eye to discover it.

First find out what the world needs and then supply that want. An invention to make smoke go the wrong way in a chimney might be a very ingenious thing, but it would be of no use to humanity. The patent office at Washington is full of wonderful devices of ingenious mechanism, but not one in hundreds is of use to the inventor or to the world. And yet how many families have been impoverished, and have struggled for years amid want and woe, while the father has been working on useless inventions.

It is estimated that five out of every seven of the millionaire manufacturers began by making with their own hands the articles which made their fortunes. One of the greatest hindrances to advancement in life is the lack of observation and of the inclination to take pains.

*   *   *

An observing barber in Newark, N. J., thought he could make an improvement in shears for cutting hair, invented clippers, and became rich. A Maine man was called in from the hayfield to wash clothes for his invalid wife. He had never realised what it was to wash before. Finding the method slow and laborious, he invented the washing-machine, and made a fortune. A man who was suffering terribly with toothache said to himself, there must be some way of filling teeth which will prevent their aching. So he invented the principle of gold filling for teeth.

The great things of the world have not been done by those of large means. Ericsson began the construction of the screw propellers in a bathroom. The cotton-gin was first manufactured in a log cabin. John Harrison, the great inventor of the marine chronometer, began his career in the loft of an old barn. Parts of the first steamboat ever run in America were set up in the vestry of a church in Philadelphia by Fitch. McCormick began to make his famous reaper in a gristmill. The first model dry dock was made in an attic. Clark, the founder of Clark University of Worcester, Mass., began his great fortune by making toy wagons in a horse shed. Farquhar made umbrellas in his sitting-room, with his daughter's help, until he sold enough to hire a loft. Edison began his experiments in a baggage car on the Grand Trunk Railroad when a newsboy.

Michael Angelo found a piece of discarded Carrara marble among waste rubbish beside a street in Florence, which some unskillful workman had cut, hacked, spoiled, and thrown away. No doubt many artists had noticed the fine quality of the marble, and regretted that it should have been spoiled. But Michael Angelo still saw an angel in the ruin, and with his chisel and mallet he called out from it one of the finest pieces of statuary in Italy, the young David.

The lonely island of Nantucket would not be considered a very favourable place to win success and fame. But Maria Mitchell, on seventy-five dollars a year, as librarian of the Nantucket Athenaeum, found time and opportunity to become a celebrated astronomer. Lucretia Mott, one of America's foremost philanthropists and reformers, who made herself felt over a whole continent, gained much of her reputation as a preacher on Nantucket Island.

*   *   *

"Why does not America have fine sculptors?" asked a romping girl, of Watertown, Mass., in 1842. Her father, a physician, answered that he supposed "an American could be a stone-cutter, but that is a very different thing from being a sculptor."

"I think," said the plucky maiden, "that if no other American tries it I will." She began her studies in Boston, and walked seven miles to and fro daily between her home and the city.

The medical schools in Boston would not admit her to study anatomy, so she had to go to St. Louis. Subsequently she went to Rome, and there, during a long residence, and afterward, modelled and carved very beautiful statuary which made the name of Harriet G. Hosmer famous.

Begin where you are; work where you are; the hour which you are now wasting, dreaming of some far-off success, may be crowded with grand possibilities.

*   *   *

There is a legend of an artist who long sought for a piece of sandalwood, out of which to carve a Madonna. He was about to give up in despair, leaving the vision of his life unrealised, when in a dream he was bidden to carve his Madonna from a block of oak wood which was destined for the fire. He obeyed, and produced a masterpiece from a log of common firewood. Many of us lose great opportunities in life by waiting to find sandalwood for our carvings, when they really lie hidden in the common logs that we burn. One woman goes through life without seeing chances for doing anything great, while another close beside her snatches from the same circumstances and privileges opportunities for achieving grand results.

Anna Dickinson began life as a school-teacher. Adelaide Neilson was a child's nurse. Charlotte Cushman's parents were poor. The renowned Jeanne d'Arc fed swine. Christine Nilsson was a poor Swedish peasant, and ran barefoot in childhood. Edmonia Lewis overcame the prejudice against her sex and colour, and pursued her profession in Italy. Maria Mitchell, the astronomer, was the daughter of a poor man who taught school at two dollars per week. These are but a few of the many who have struggled with fate and risen to distinction through their own personal efforts.

Opportunities? They are everywhere. Never before were there such grand openings, such chances, such opportunities. Especially is this true for girls and young women. A new era is dawning for them. Hundreds of occupations and professions, which were closed to them only a few years ago, are now inviting them to enter.

We cannot all of us perhaps make great discoveries like Newton, Faraday, Edison, and Thompson. We cannot all of us paint immortal pictures like an Angelo or a Raphael. But we can all of us make our lives sublime, by seizing common occasions and making them great. What chance had the young girl, Grace Darling, to distinguish herself, living on those barren lighthouse rocks alone with her aged parents? But while her brothers and sisters, who moved to the cities to win wealth and fame, are not known to the world, she became more famous than a princess. This poor girl did not need to go to London to see the nobility; they came to the lighthouse to see her. Right at home this young girl had won fame which the regal heirs might envy, and a name which will never perish from the earth. She did not wander away into dreamy distance for fame and fortune, but did her best where duty had placed her.

If you want to get rich, study yourself and your own wants. You will find that millions have the same wants. The safest business is always connected with prime necessities. A woman must have clothing and a dwelling; she must eat. She wants comforts, facilities of all kinds for pleasure, luxuries, education, and culture. Any woman who can supply a great want of humanity, improve any methods which people use, supply any demand of comfort, or contribute in any way to their well-being, can make a fortune.

*   *   *

The golden opportunity
Is never offered twice; seize then the hour
When fortune smiles and duty points the way;
Nor shrink aside to 'scape the spectre fear,
Nor pause, though pleasure beckon from her bower;
But bravely bear thee onward to the goal.
ANON.

For the distant still thou yearnest,
And behold the good so near;
If to use the good thou learnest,
Thou wilt surely find it here.
GOETHE.

Do not, then, stand idly waiting
For some greater work to do;
Fortune is a lazy goddess—
She will never come to you.
Go and toil in any vineyard,
Do not fear to do or dare;
If you want a field of labor,
You can find it anywhere.
ELLEN H. GATES.

Why thus longing, thus forever sighing,
For the far-off, unattained and dim,
While the beautiful, all around thee lying
Offers up its low, perpetual hymn?
HARRIET WINSLOW.

Work for the good that is nighest;

Dream not of greatness afar:
That glory is ever the highest
Which shines upon men as they are.
W. MORLEY PUNSHON.

THE MIGHT OF LITTLE THINGS

Little strokes fell great oaks.—FRANKLIN.

Think naught a trifle, though it small appear;
Small sands the mountain, moments make the year,
And trifles, life.
YOUNG.

"Scorn not the slightest word or deed,
Nor deem it void of power;
There's fruit in each wind-wafted seed,
That waits its natal hour."

Often from our weakness our strongest principles of conduct are born;
and from the acorn, which a breeze has wafted, springs the oak which
defies the storm.—BULWER.

The creation of a thousand forests is in one acorn.—EMERSON.

"A pebble on the streamlet scant
Has turned the course of many a river;
A dewdrop on the baby plant
Has warped the giant oak forever."

The mother of mischief is no bigger than a midge's wing.—SCOTCH
PROVERB.

*   *   *

Trifles light as air often suggest to the thinking mind ideas which have revolutionised the world.

Sometimes a conversation, or a sentence in a letter, or a paragraph in an article, will help us to reproduce the whole character of the author; as a single bone, a fish scale, a fin, or a tooth, will enable the scientist and anatomist to reproduce the fish or the animal, although extinct for ages.

Among the lofty Alps, it is said, the guides sometimes demand absolute silence, lest the vibration of the voice bring down an avalanche.

*   *   *

The power of observation in the American Indian would put many an educated man to shame. Returning home, an Indian discovered that his venison, which had been hanging up to dry, had been stolen. After careful observation he started to track the thief through the woods. Meeting a man on the route, he asked him if he had seen a little, old, white man, with a short gun, and with a small bob-tailed dog. The man told him he had met such a man, but was surprised to find that the Indian had not even seen the one he described. He asked the Indian how he could give such a minute description of the man whom he had never seen. "I knew the thief was a little man," said the Indian, "because he rolled up a stone to stand on in order to reach the venison; I knew he was an old man by his short steps; I knew he was a white man by his turning out his toes in walking, which an Indian never does; I knew he had a short gun by the mark it left on the tree where he had stood it up; I knew the dog was small by his tracks and short steps, and that he had a bob-tail by the mark it left in the dust where he sat."

*   *   *

Two drops of rain, falling side by side, were separated a few inches by a gentle breeze. Striking on opposite sides of the roof of a court-house in Wisconsin, one rolled southward through the Rock River and the Mississippi to the Gulf of Mexico; while the other entered successively the Fox River, Green Bay, Lake Michigan, the Straits of Mackinaw, Lake Huron, St. Clair River, Lake St. Clair, Detroit River, Lake Erie, Niagara River, Lake Ontario, the St. Lawrence River, and finally reached the Gulf of St. Lawrence. How slight the influence of the breeze, yet such was the formation of the continent that a trifling cause was multiplied almost beyond the power of figures to express its momentous effect upon the destinies of these companion raindrops. Who can calculate the future of the smallest trifle when a mud crack swells to an Amazon, and the stealing of a penny may end on the scaffold? Who does not know that the act of a moment may cause a life's regret? A trigger may be pulled in an instant, but the soul returns never.

A spark falling upon some combustibles led to the invention of gunpowder. A few bits of seaweed and driftwood, floating on the waves, enabled Columbus to stay a mutiny of his sailors which threatened to prevent the discovery of a new world. There are moments in history which balance years of ordinary life. Dana could interest a class for hours on a grain of sand; and from a single bone, such as no one had ever seen before, Agassiz could deduce the entire structure and habits of an animal so accurately that subsequent discoveries of complete skeletons have not changed one of his conclusions.

A cricket once saved a military expedition from destruction. The commanding officer and hundreds of his men were going to South America on a great ship, and, through the carelessness of the watch, they would have been dashed upon a ledge of rock had it not been for a cricket which a soldier had brought on board. When the little insect scented the land, it broke its long silence by a shrill note, and this warned them of their danger.

By gnawing through a dike, even a rat may drown a nation. A little boy in Holland saw water trickling from a small hole near the bottom of a dike. He realised that the leak would rapidly become larger if the water was not checked, so he held his hand over the hole for hours on a dark and dismal night until he could attract the attention of passers-by. His name is still held in grateful remembrance in Holland.

*　　*　　*

The beetling chalk cliffs of England were built by rhizopods, too small to be clearly seen without the aid of a magnifying-glass.

What was so unlikely as that throwing an empty wine-flask in the fire should furnish the first notion of a locomotive, or that the sickness of an Italian chemist's wife and her absurd craving for reptiles for food should begin the electric telegraph?

Madame Galvani noticed the contraction of the muscles of a skinned frog which was accidentally touched at the moment her husband took a spark from an electrical machine. She gave the hint which led to the discovery of galvanic electricity, now so useful in the arts and in transmitting vocal or written language.

*　　*　　*

Congress met near a livery stable to discuss the Declaration of Independence. The members, in knee breeches and silk stockings, were so annoyed by flies, which they could not keep away with their handkerchiefs, that it has been said they cut short the debate, and hastened to affix their signatures to the greatest document in history.

"The fate of a nation," says Gladstone, "has often depended upon the good or bad digestion of a fine dinner."

A young man once went to India to seek his fortune, but, finding no opening, he went to his room, loaded his pistol, put the muzzle to his head, and pulled the trigger. But it did not go off. He went to the window to point it in another direction and try it again, resolved that if the weapon went off he would regard it as a Providence that he was spared. He pulled the trigger and it went off the first time. Trembling with excitement he resolved to hold his life sacred, to make the most of it, and never again to cheapen it. This young man became General Robert Clive, who, with but a handful of European soldiers, secured to the East India Company and afterwards to Great Britain a great and rich country with two hundred millions of people.

The cackling of a goose aroused the sentinels and saved Rome from the Gauls, and the pain from a thistle warned a Scottish army of the approach of the Danes.

*　　*　　*

In the earliest days of cotton spinning, the small fibres would stick to the bobbins, and make it necessary to stop and clear the machinery. Although this loss of time reduced the earnings of the operatives, the father of Robert Peel noticed that one of his spinners always drew full pay, as his machine never stopped. "How is this, Dick?" asked Mr. Peel one day; "the on-looker tells me your bobbins are always clean."

"Ay, that they be," replied Dick Ferguson.

"How do you manage it, Dick?"

"Why, you see, Meester Peel," said the workman, "it is sort o' secret! If I

124

tow'd ye, yo'd be as wise as I am."

"That's so," said Mr. Peel, smiling; "but I'd give you something to know. Could you make all the looms work as smoothly as yours?"

"Ivery one of 'em, meester," replied Dick.

"Well, what shall I give you for your secret?" asked Mr. Peel, and Dick replied, "Gi' me a quart of ale every day as I'm in the mills, and I'll tell thee all about it."

"Agreed," said Mr. Peel, and Dick whispered very cautiously in his ear, "Chalk your bobbins!" That was the whole secret, and Mr. Peel soon shot ahead of all his competitors, for he made machines that would chalk their own bobbins. Dick was handsomely rewarded with money instead of beer. His little idea has saved the world millions of dollars.

* * *

A famous ruby was offered to the English government. The report of the crown jeweller was that it was the finest he had ever seen or heard of, but that one of the "facets" was slightly fractured. That invisible fracture reduced its value thousands of dollars, and it was rejected from the regalia of England.

It was a little thing for the janitor to leave a lamp swinging in the cathedral at Pisa, but in that steady swaying motion the boy Galileo saw the pendulum, and conceived the idea of thus measuring time.

"I was singing to the mouthpiece of a telephone," said Edison, "when the vibrations of my voice caused a fine steel point to pierce one of my fingers held just behind it. That set me to thinking. If I could record the motions of the point and send it over the same surface afterward, I saw no reason why the thing would not talk. I determined to make a machine that would work accurately, and gave my assistants the necessary instructions, telling them what I had discovered. That's the whole story. The phonograph is the result of the pricking of a finger."

* * *

It was a little thing for a cow to kick over a lantern left in a shanty, but it laid Chicago in ashes, and rendered homeless a hundred thousand people.

You turned a cold shoulder but once, you made but one stinging remark, yet it lost you a friend forever.

Some little weakness, some self-indulgence, a quick temper, lack of decisiveness, are little things, you say, when placed beside great abilities, but they have wrecked many a career. The Parliament of Great Britain, the Congress of the United States, and representative governments all over the world have come from King John signing the Magna Charta.

The sight of a stranded cuttlefish led Cuvier to an investigation which made him one of the greatest natural historians in the world. The web of a spider suggested to Captain Brown the idea of a suspension bridge. A man, looking for a lost horse, picked up a stone in the Idaho mountains which led to the discovery of a rich gold mine.

*   *   *

"I cannot see that you have made any progress since my last visit," said a gentleman to Michael Angelo.

"But," said the sculptor, "I have retouched this part, polished that, softened that feature, brought out that muscle, given some expression to this lip, more energy to that limb, etc."

"But they are trifles!" exclaimed the visitor.

"It may be so," replied the great artist, "but trifles make perfection, and perfection is no trifle."

That infinite patience which made Michael Angelo spend a week in bringing out a muscle in a statue with more vital fidelity to truth, or Gerhard Dow a day in giving the right effect to a dewdrop on a cabbage leaf, makes all the difference between success and failure.

*   *   *

By scattering it upon a sloping field of grain so as to form, in letters of great size, "Effects of Gypsum," Franklin brought this fertiliser into general use in America. By means of a kite he established principles in the science of electricity of such broad significance that they underlie nearly all the modern applications of that science, with probably boundless possibilities of development in the future.

126

More than four hundred and fifty years have passed since Laurens Coster amused his children by cutting their names in the bark of trees, in the land of windmills, and the monks have laid aside forever their old trade of copying books. As he carved the names of his prattling children it occurred to him that if the letters were made in separate blocks, and wet with ink, they would make clear printed impressions better and more rapidly than would the pen. So he made blocks, tied them together with strings, and printed a pamphlet with the aid of a hired man, John Gutenberg. People bought the pamphlets at a slight reduction from the price charged by the monks, supposing that the work was done in the old way. Coster died soon afterward, but young Gutenberg kept the secret, and experimented with metals until he had invented the metal type. In an obscure chamber in Strasburg he printed his first book.

At about this time a traveler called upon Charles VII. of France, who was so afraid somebody would poison him that he dared eat but little, and made his servants taste of every dish of food before he ate any. He looked with suspicion upon the stranger; but when the latter offered a beautiful copy of the Bible for only seven hundred and fifty crowns, the monarch bought it at once. Charles showed his Bible to the archbishop, telling him that it was the finest copy in the world, without a blot or mistake, and that it must have taken the copyist a lifetime to write it. "Why!" exclaimed the archbishop in surprise, "I bought one exactly like it a few days ago." It was soon learned that other rich people in Paris had bought similar copies. The king traced the book to John Faust, of Strasburg, who had furnished Gutenberg money to experiment with. The people said that Faust must have sold himself to the devil, and he only escaped burning at the stake by divulging the secret.

*   *   *

The cry of the infant Moses attracted the attention of Pharaoh's daughter, and gave the Jews a lawgiver. A bird alighting on the bough of a tree at the mouth of the cave where Mahomet lay hid turned aside his pursuers, and gave a prophet to many nations. A flight of birds probably prevented Columbus from discovering this continent, for when he was growing anxious, Martin Alonzo Pinzon persuaded him to follow a flight of parrots toward the southwest; for to the Spanish seamen of that day it was good luck to follow in the wake of a flock of birds when on a voyage of discovery. But for his change of course Columbus would have reached the coast of Florida. "Never," wrote Humboldt, "had the flight of birds more important consequences."

The children of a spectacle-maker placed two or more pairs of the spectacles before each other in play, and told their father that distant objects looked larger. From this hint came the telescope.

"Of what use is it?" people asked with a sneer, when Franklin told of his discovery that lightning and electricity are identical. "What is the use of a child?" replied Franklin; "it may become an adult."

*   *   *

"He who waits to do a great deal of good at once," said Dr. Johnson, "will never do any." Do good with what thou hast, or it will do thee no good.

Every day is a little life; and our whole life but a day repeated. Those that dare lose a day are dangerously prodigal, those that dare misspend it, desperate. What is the happiness of your life made up of? Little courtesies, little kindnesses, pleasant words, genial smiles, a friendly letter, good wishes, and good deeds. One in a million—once in a lifetime—may do a heroic action. The atomic theory is the true one. Many think common fractions vulgar, but they are the components of millions.

It is a great woman who sees great things where others see little things, who sees the extraordinary in the ordinary.

How many a lawyer has failed from the lack of details in deeds and important papers, the lack of little words which seemed like surplus, and which involved her clients in litigation, and often great losses! How many wills are contested from the carelessness of lawyers in the omission or shading of words, or ambiguous use of language!

Physicians often fail to make a reputation through their habitual blundering, carelessness in writing prescriptions, failure to give minute instruction.

*   *   *

Not even Helen of Troy, it is said, was beautiful enough to spare the tip of her nose; and if Cleopatra's had been an inch shorter Mark Antony would never have become infatuated with her wonderful charms, and the blemish would have changed the history of the world. Anne Boleyn's fascinating smile split the great Church of Rome in half, and gave a nation an altered destiny. Napoleon, who feared not to attack the proudest

128

monarchs in their capitols, shrank from the political influence of one independent woman in private life, Madame de Staël.

Cromwell was about to sail for America when a law was passed prohibiting emigration. At that time he was a profligate, having squandered all his property. But when he found that he could not leave England he reformed his life. Had he not been detained who can tell what the history of Great Britain would have been?

It was the little foxes that spoiled the vines in Solomon's day. Mites play mischief now with our meal and cheese, moths with our woollens and furs, and mice in our pantries. More than half our diseases are produced by minute viruses and bacteria.

*   *   *

Most people call fretting a minor fault, a foible, and not a vice. There is no vice except drunkenness which can so utterly destroy the peace, the happiness, of a home.

"We call the large majority of human lives obscure," says Bulwer, "presumptuous that we are! How know we what lives a single thought retained from the dust of nameless graves may have lighted to renown?"

"Behold how great a matter a little fire kindleth."

"A look of vexation or a word coldly spoken, or a little help thoughtlessly withheld, may produce long issues of regret."

It was but a little dispute, a little flash of temper, the trigger was pulled in an instant, but the soul returned never.

*   *   *

"For want of a nail the shoe was lost,
For want of a shoe the horse was lost;
For want of a horse the rider was lost, and all."

*   *   *

"Do little things now," says a Persian proverb; "so shall big things come to thee by and by asking to be done." God will take care of the great things if we do not neglect the little ones.

"Words are things," says Byron, "and a small drop of ink, falling like dew upon a thought, produces that which makes thousands, perhaps millions think."

"I give these books for the founding of a college in this colony;" such were the words of ten ministers who in the year 1700 assembled at the village of Branford a few miles east of New Haven. Each of the worthy fathers deposited a few books upon the table around which they were sitting; such was the founding of Yale College.

The pyramid of knowledge is made up of little grains of information, little observations picked up from everywhere.

*   *   *

Great women are noted for their attention to trifles. "The eye of the understanding is like the eye of the sense; for as you may see objects through small crannies or holes, so you may see great axioms of nature through small and contemptible instances," said Bacon. Trifles light as air suggest to the keen observer the solution of mighty problems. Bits of glass arranged to amuse children led to the discovery of the kaleidoscope. Goodyear discovered how to vulcanise rubber by forgetting, until it became red hot, a skillet containing a compound which was considered worthless. Confined in the house by typhoid fever, Helmholtz, with a little money which he had saved by great economy, bought a microscope which led him into the field of science where he became so famous. A ship-worm boring a piece of wood suggested to Sir Isambard Brunei the idea of a tunnel under the Thames at London. Tracks of extinct animals in the old red sandstone led Hugh Miller on and on until he became the greatest geologist of his time. Sir Walter Scott once saw a shepherd boy plodding sturdily along, and asked him to ride. This boy was George Kemp, who became so enthusiastic in his study of sculpture that he walked fifty miles and back to see a beautiful statue. He did not forget the kindness of Sir Walter, and, when the latter died, threw his soul into the design of the magnificent monument erected in Edinburgh to the memory of the author of "Waverley."

It was the turning point in Theodore Parker's life when he picked up a stone to throw at a turtle. Something within him said, "Don't do it," and he didn't. He went home and asked his mother what it was in him that said "Don't;" and she taught him the purpose of that inward monitor which he ever after chose as his guide. Voltaire could not erase from his mind the impression of a poem on infidelity committed at the age of five. The

"Arabian Nights" aroused the genius of Coleridge. A Massachusetts soldier in the Civil War observed a bird hulling rice, and shot it; taking its bill for a model, he invented a hulling machine which has revolutionized the rice business. A war between France and England, costing more than a hundred thousand lives, grew out of a quarrel as to which of two vessels should first be served with water. The quarrel of two Indian boys over a grasshopper led to the "Grasshopper War." George IV. of England fell in a fit, and a village apothecary bled him, restoring him to consciousness. The king made him his physician, a position of great honour and profit.

No object the eye ever beheld, no sound however slight caught by the ear, or anything once passing the turnstile of any of the senses, is ever let go. The eye is a perpetual camera imprinting upon the sensitive mental plates, and packing away in the brain for future use every face, every tree, every plant, flower, hill, stream, mountain, every scene upon the street, in fact, everything which comes within its range. There is a phonograph in our natures which catches, however thoughtless and transient, every syllable we utter, and registers forever the slightest enunciation, and renders it immortal. These notes may appear a thousand years hence, reproduced in our descendants, in all their beautiful or terrible detail.

*   *   *

All the ages that have been are rounded up into the small space we call "Today." Every life spans all that precedes it. Today is a book which contains everything that has transpired in the world up to the present moment. The millions of the past whose ashes have mingled with the dust for centuries still live in their destinies through the laws of heredity.

Nothing has ever been lost. All the infinitesimals of the past are amassed into the present.

The first acorn had wrapped up in it all the oak forests on the globe.

"Least of all seeds, greatest of all harvests," seems to be one of the great laws of nature. All life comes from microscopic beginnings. In nature there is nothing small. The microscope reveals as great a world below as the telescope above. All of nature's laws govern the smallest atoms, and a single drop of water is a miniature ocean.

*   *   *

The strength of a chain lies in its weakest link, however large and strong all the others may be. We are all inclined to be proud of our strong points, while we are sensitive and neglectful of our weaknesses. Yet it is our greatest weakness which measures our real strength. A soldier who escapes the bullets of a thousand battles may die from the scratch of a pin, and many a ship has survived the shocks of icebergs and the storms of ocean only to founder in a smooth sea from holes made by tiny insects. Drop by drop is instilled into the mind the poison which blasts many a precious life.

How often do we hear people say, "Oh, it's only ten minutes, or twenty minutes, till dinner time; there's no use doing anything," or use other expressions of a like effect? Why, it is just in these little spare bits of time, these odd moments, which most people throw away, that women who have risen have gained their education, written their books, and made themselves immortal.

Small things become great when a great soul sees them. The noble or heroic act of one woman has sometimes elevated a nation. Many an honourable career has resulted from a kind word spoken in season or the warm grasp of a friendly hand.

*   *   *

It is the little rift within the lute,
That by and by will make the music mute,
And, ever widening, slowly silence all.
TENNYSON.

"It was only a glad 'good-morning,'
As she passed along the way,
But it spread the morning's glory
Over the livelong day."

"Only a thought in passing—a smile, or encouraging word,
Has lifted many a burden no other gift could have stirred.
Only!—But then the onlys
Make up the mighty all."

SELF MASTERY

Strength of character consists of two things,—power of will and power of self-restraint. It requires two things, therefore, for its existence,—strong feelings and strong command over them.—F. W. ROBERTSON.

"Self-reverence, self-knowledge, self-control,
These three alone lead life to sovereign power."

Real glory springs from the conquest of ourselves; and without that the conqueror is naught but the veriest slave.—
THOMSON.

Whatever day makes [wo]man a slave takes half [her] worth away.—
ODYSSEY.

Self-trust is of the essence of heroism.—EMERSON.

*   *   *

"Ah! Diamond, you little know the mischief you have wrought," said Sir Isaac Newton, returning from supper to find that his dog had upset a lighted taper upon the laborious calculations of years, which lay in ashes before him. Then he went calmly to work to reproduce them. The man who thus excelled in self-mastery surpassed all his predecessors and contemporaries in mastering the laws of nature.

The sun was high in the heavens when a man called at the house of

Pericles to abuse him. The man's anger knew no bounds. He vented his spite in violent language until he paused from sheer exhaustion, and saw that it was quite dark without. He turned to go home, when Pericles calmly called a servant, and said, "Bring a lamp and attend this man home." Is any argument needed to show the superiority of Pericles?

The American Minister at St. Petersburg was summoned one morning to save a young, dissolute, reckless American youth, Poe, from the penalties incurred in a drunken debauch. By the Minister's aid young Poe returned to the United States. Not long after this the author of the best story and poem competed for in the "Baltimore Visitor" was sent for, and behold, the youth who had taken both prizes was that same dissolute, reckless, penniless, orphan youth, who had been arrested in St. Petersburg,—pale, ragged, with no stockings, and with his threadbare but well brushed coat buttoned to the chin to conceal the lack of a shirt. Young Poe took fresh courage and resolution, and for a while showed that he was superior to the appetite which was striving to drag him down. But, alas, that fatal bottle! his mind was stored with riches, yet he died in moral poverty. This was a soldier's epitaph:—

"Here lies a soldier whom all must applaud,
Who fought many battles at home and abroad!
But the hottest engagement he ever was in,
Was the conquest of self, in the battle of sin."

*　　*　　*

"The first and best of victories," says Plato, "is for a man to conquer himself; to be conquered by himself is, of all things, the most shameful and vile."

Self-control is at the root of all the virtues. Let a woman yield to her impulses and passions, and from that moment she gives up her moral freedom.

"Teach self-denial and make its practice pleasurable," says Walter Scott, "and you create for the world a destiny more sublime than ever issued from the brain of the wildest dreamer."

Stonewall Jackson, early in life, determined to conquer every weakness he had, physical, mental, and moral. He held all of his powers with a firm hand. To his great self-discipline and self-mastery he owed his success. So determined was he to harden himself to the weather that he could not be induced to wear an overcoat in winter. "I will not give in to the cold," he said. For a year, on account of dyspepsia, he lived on buttermilk and stale bread, and wore a wet shirt next his body because his doctor advised it, although everybody else ridiculed the idea. This was while he was professor at the Virginia Military Institute. His doctor advised him to retire at nine o'clock; and, no matter where he was, or who was present, he always sought his bed on the minute. He adhered rigidly through life to this stern system of discipline. Such self-training, such self-conquest, gives one great power over others. It is equal to genius itself.

*   *   *

It is a good plan to form the habit of ranking our various qualities, marking our strongest point one hundred and all the others in proportion, in order to make the lowest mark more apparent, and enabling us to try to raise or strengthen it. A woman's industry, for example, may be her strongest point, one hundred, her physical courage may be fifty; her moral courage, seventy-five; her temper, twenty-five; with but ten for self-control,—which, if she has strong appetites and passions, will be likely to be the rock on which she will split. A woman should strive in every way to raise it from one of the weakest qualities to one of the strongest. It would take but two or three minutes a day to rank ourselves in such a table by noting the exercise of each faculty for the day. If you have worked hard and faithfully, mark industry one hundred. If you have lost your temper, and, in consequence, lost your self-control, and made a fool of yourself, indicate it by a low mark. This will be an incentive to try to raise it the next day. If you have been irritable, indicate it by a corresponding mark, and redeem yourself on the morrow. If you have been cowardly where you should have been brave, hesitating where you should have shown decision, false where you should have been true, foolish where you should have been wise, tardy where you should have been prompt; if you have prevaricated where you should have told the exact truth; if you have taken the advantage where you should have been fair, have been unjust where you should have been just, impatient where you should have been patient, cross where you should have been cheerful, so indicate by your marks. You will find this a great aid to character building.

*   *   *

It is a subtle and profound remark of Hegel's that the riddle which the Sphinx, the Egyptian symbol of the mysteriousness of Nature, propounds to Oedipus is only another way of expressing the command of the Delphic oracle, "Know thyself." And when the answer is given the Sphinx casts herself down from her rock. When a woman knows herself, the mysteriousness of Nature and her terrors vanish.

The command by the ancient oracle at Delphos is of eternal significance. Add to it its natural complement—Help thyself—and the path to success is open to those who obey.

Guard your weak point. Moral contagion borrows fully half its strength from the weakness of its victims. Have you a hot, passionate temper? If so, a moment's outbreak, like a rat-hole in a dam, may flood all the work of years. One angry word sometimes raises a storm that time itself cannot allay. A single angry word has lost many a friend.

*　　*　　*

When Socrates found in himself any disposition to anger, he would check it by speaking low, in opposition to the motions of his displeasure. If you are conscious of being in a rage, keep your mouth shut, lest you increase it. Many a person has dropped dead in a rage. "Whom the gods would destroy they first make mad." "Be calm in arguing," says George Herbert, "for fierceness makes error a fault, and truth discourtesy."

To be angry with a weak man is to prove that you are not strong yourself. "Anger," says Pythagoras, "begins with folly and ends with repentance." You must measure the strength of a woman by the power of the feelings she subdues, not by the power of those which subdue her.

De Leon, a distinguished Spanish poet, after lying years in dungeons of the Inquisition, dreary, and alone, without light, for translating part of the Scriptures into his native tongue, was released and restored to his professorship. A great crowd thronged to hear his first lecture, out of curiosity to learn what he might say about his imprisonment. But the great man merely resumed the lecture which had been so cruelly broken off five years before, just where he left it, with the words "Heri discebamus" (Yesterday we were teaching). What a lesson in this remarkable example of self-control for those who allow their tongues to jabber whatever happens to be uppermost in their minds!

That woman has conquered her tongue who can allow the retort or snipey reply to die unspoken on her lips, and maintain an indignant silence amid reproaches and accusations and sneers and scoffs.

*　　*　　*

136

Peter the Great made a law in 1722 that a nobleman who should beat his slave should be regarded as insane, and a guardian appointed to look after his property and person. This great monarch once struck his gardener, who took to his bed and died. Peter, hearing of this, exclaimed with tears in his eyes, "Alas! I have civilised my own subjects; I have conquered other nations; yet have I not been able to civilise or conquer myself." The same monarch, when drunk, rushed upon Admiral Le Fort with a sword. Le Fort, with great self-possession, bared his breast to receive the stroke. This sobered Peter, and afterwards he asked the pardon of Le Fort. Peter said, "I am trying to reform my country, and I am not yet able to reform myself." Self-conquest is man's last and greatest victory.

It was the self-discipline of a man who had never looked upon war until he was forty that enabled Oliver Cromwell to create an army which never fought without annihilating, yet which retired into the ranks of industry as soon as the government was established, each soldier being distinguished from his neighbours only by his superior diligence, sobriety, and regularity in the pursuits of peace.

How sweet the serenity of habitual self-command! When does a woman feel more a master of herself than when she has passed through a sudden and severe provocation in silence or in undisturbed good humour?

*   *   *

Whether teaching the rules of an exact morality, answering his corrupt judges, receiving sentence of death, or swallowing the poison, Socrates was still calm, quiet, undisturbed, intrepid.

It is a great thing to have brains, but it is vastly greater to be able to command them. The Duke of Wellington had great power over himself, although his natural temper was extremely irritable. He remained at the Duchess of Richmond's ball till about three o'clock on the morning of the 16th of June, 1815, "showing himself very cheerful," although he knew that a desperate battle was awaiting him. On the field of Waterloo he gave his orders at the most critical moments without the slightest excitement.

"He that would govern others first should be
The master of himself," says Massinger.

He who has mastered himself, who is his own Caesar, will be stronger than his passion, superior to circumstances, higher than his calling, greater than his speech. Self-control is the generalship which turns a mob of raw recruits into a disciplined army. The rough man has become the polished and dignified soldier, in other words, the man has got control of himself, and knows how to use himself. The human race is under constant drill. Our occupations, difficulties, obstacles, disappointments, if used aright, are the great schoolmasters which help us to possess ourselves. The woman who is master of herself will not be a slave to drudgery, but will keep in advance of her work. She will not rob her family of that which is worth more than money or position; she will not be the slave of her occupation, not at the mercy of circumstances. Her methods and system will enable her to accomplish wonders, and yet give her leisure for self-culture. **The woman who controls herself works to live rather than lives for work.**

*　　*　　*

The woman of great self-control, the woman who thinks a great deal and says little, who is self-centred, well balanced, carries a thousand times more weight than the woman of weak will, always wavering and undecided.

If a woman lacks self-control she seems to lack everything. Without it she can have no patience, no power to govern herself, she can have no self-reliance, for she will always be at the mercy of her strongest passion. If she lacks self-control, the very backbone, pith, and nerve of character are lacking also.

The discipline which is the main end in education is simply control acquired over one's mental faculties; without this discipline no woman is a strong and accurate thinker. "Prove to me," says Mrs. Oliphant, "that you can control yourself, and I'll say you're an educated woman; and, without this, all other education is good for next to nothing."

*　　*　　*

The wife of Socrates, Xanthippe, was a woman of a most fantastical and furious spirit. At one time, having vented all the reproaches upon Socrates her fury could suggest, he went out and sat before the door. His calm and unconcerned behaviour but irritated her so much the more; and, in the excess of her rage, she ran upstairs and emptied a vessel upon his head, at which he only laughed and said that "so much thunder must needs produce a shower." Alcibiades his friend, talking with him about his wife, told him he wondered how he could bear such an everlasting scold in the same house with him. He replied, "I have so accustomed myself to expect it, that it now offends me no more than the noise of carriages in the street."

How many women have in their chain of character one weak link. They may be weak in the link of truthfulness, politeness, trustworthiness, temper, temperance, courage, industry, or may have some other weakness which wrecks their success and thwarts a life's endeavour. She who would succeed must hold all her faculties under perfect control; they must be disciplined, drilled, until they obey the will.

Seneca, one of the greatest of the ancient philosophers, said that "we should every night call ourselves to account. What infirmity have I mastered today? what passion opposed? what temptation resisted? what virtue acquired?" and then he follows with the profound truth that "our vices will abate of themselves if they be brought every day to the shrift." If you cannot at first control your anger, learn to control your tongue, which, like fire, is a good servant, but a hard master.

Half the actual trouble of life would be saved if people would remember that silence is golden, when they are irritated, vexed, or annoyed.

*   *   *

To feel provoked or exasperated at a trifle, when the nerves are exhausted, is, perhaps, natural to us in our imperfect state. But why put into the shape of speech the annoyance which, once uttered, is remembered; which may burn like a blistering wound, or rankle like a poisoned arrow? If a child be crying or a friend capricious, or a servant unreasonable, be careful what you say. Do not speak while you feel the impulse of anger, for you will be almost certain to say too much, to say more than your cooler judgment will approve, and to speak in a way that you will regret. Be silent until the "sweet by and by," when you will be calm, rested, and self-controlled.

"Silence," says Zimmerman, "is the safest response for all the contradiction that arises from impertinence, vulgarity, or envy."

The self-controlled are self-possessed.

*   *   *

Experience shows that, quicker than almost any other physical agency, alcohol breaks down a woman's power of self-control. But the physical evils of intemperance, great as they are, are slight, compared with the moral injury it produces. It is not simply that vices and crimes almost inevitably follow the loss of rational self-direction, which is the invariable accompaniment of intoxication; manhood is lowered and finally lost by the sensual tyranny of appetite. The drunken woman has given up the reins of her nature to a fool or a fiend, and she is driven fast to base or unutterably foolish ends.

Natural appetites, if given rein, will not only grow monstrous and despotic, but artificial appetites will be created which, like a ghastly Frankenstein, develop a kind of independent life and force, and then turn on their creator to torment him without pity, and will mock his efforts to free himself from this slavery. The victim of strong drink is one of the most pitiable creatures on earth, he becomes half beast, or half demon. Oh, the silent, suffering tongues that whisper "Don't," but the will lies prostrate, and the debauch goes on. What a mute confession of degradation there is in the very appearance of a confirmed sot. Behold a man no longer in possession of himself; the flesh is master; the spiritual nature is sunk in the mire of sensuality, and the mental faculties are a mere mob of enfeebled powers under bondage to a bestial or mad tyrant. As Challis says:—

"Once the demon enters,
Stands within the door;
Peace and hope and gladness
Dwell there nevermore."

*   *   *

Many persons are intemperate in their feelings; they are emotionally prodigal. Passion is intemperance; so is caprice. There is an intemperance even in melancholy and mirth. The temperate woman is not mastered by her moods; she will not be driven or enticed into excess; her steadfast will conquers despondency, and is not unbalanced by transient exhilarations, for ecstasy is as fatal as despair. Temper is subjected to reason and conscience. How many people excuse themselves for doing wrong or foolish acts by the plea that they have a quick temper. But she who is ruler of herself rules her temper, turning its very heat and passion into energy that works good instead of evil.

George Washington's faculties were so well balanced and combined that his constitution was tempered evenly with all the elements of activity, and his mind resembled a well organised commonwealth. His passions, which had the intensest vigour, owed allegiance to reason; and with all the fiery quickness of his spirit, his impetuous and massive will was held in check by consummate judgment. He had in his composition a calm which was a balance-wheel, and which gave him in moments of highest excitement the power of self-control, and enabled him to excel in patience, even when he had most cause for disgust.

It was said by an enemy of William the Silent that an arrogant or indiscreet word never fell from his lips.

A self-controlled mind is a free mind, and freedom is power.

*　*　*

"It is not enough to have great qualities," says La Rochefoucauld; "we should also have the management of them." No woman can call herself educated until every voluntary muscle obeys her will.

Every human being is conscious of two natures. One is ever reaching up after the good, the true, and the noble,—is aspiring after all that uplifts, elevates, and purifies. The other is the bestial side which gravitates downward. It does not aspire, it grovels; it wallows in the mire of sensualism. Like the beast, it knows but one law, and is led by only one motive, self-indulgence, self-gratification. When neither hungry nor thirsty, or when gorged and sated by over-indulgence, it lies quiet and peaceful as a lamb, and we sometimes think it subdued. But when its imperious passion accumulates, it clamours for satisfaction. You cannot reason with it, for it has no reason, only an imperious instinct for gratification. You cannot appeal to its self-respect, for it has none. It cares nothing for character, for manliness, for the spiritual.

These two natures are ever at war, one pulling heavenward, the other, earthward. Nor do they ever become reconciled. Either may conquer, but the vanquished never submits. The higher nature may be compelled to grovel, to wallow in the mire of sensual indulgence, but it always rebels and enters its protest. The still small voice which bids woman look up is never quite hushed. If the victim of the lower nature could only forget that she was born to look upward, if she could only hush the voice which haunts her and condemns her when she is bound in slavery, if she could only enjoy her indulgences without the mockery of remorse, she thinks she would be content to remain a slave. But the ghost of her better self rises as she is about to partake of her delight, and robs her of the expected pleasure. She has sold her better self for pleasure which is poison, and she cannot lose the consciousness of the fearful sacrifice she has made.

*　*　*

Give me that soul, superior power,

141

That conquest over fate,
Which sways the weakness of the hour,
Rules little things as great:
That lulls the human waves of strife
With words and feelings kind,
And makes the trials of our life
The triumphs of our mind.
CHARLES SWAIN.

I have only one counsel for you—Be master.—NAPOLEON.

Ah, silly man, who dream'st thy honor stands
In ruling others, not thyself. Thy slaves
Serve thee, and thou thy slave: in iron bands
Thy servile spirit, pressed with wild passions, raves.
Wouldst thou live honored?—clip ambition's wing:
To reason's yoke thy furious passions bring:
Thrice noble is the man who of himself is king.
PHINEAS FLETCHER.

"Not in the clamor of the crowded street,
Not in the shouts and plaudits of the throng,
But in ourselves are triumph and defeat."

He that is slow to anger is better than the mighty: and he that ruleth his spirit than he that taketh a city.—BIBLE.

ABOUT THE AUTHOR

Jacqui Brauman is the principal solicitor of TBA Law, and has owned the firm for nearly 4 years. She has a Bachelor of Laws, Bachelor of Accounting, Advanced Diploma in Taxation Law, and a Masters in Applied Law (Wills and Estates).

Practicing mainly in wills and estates, and property law, Jacqui's career of 10 years has taken her from Central Victoria to rural New South Wales, to Sydney, and back to the outskirts of Melbourne.

Jacqui is now beginning her transition out of law and toward becoming a full time writer of both fiction and non-fiction. Her diary of this process can be found at HaveItAll.net.au and she can be contacted at jacqui@haveitall.net.au

Public school educated and raised in Wangaratta, Jacqui is married to Daniel who is a serving member in the Royal Australian Army. This live together with their blue-heeler at their property just south of Seymour. Together they do plenty of adventurous sports, including motorcycling, kayaking, camping, 4x4 and fishing. Jacqui also enjoys distance running and generally keeping fit.

www.ingramcontent.com/pod-product-compliance
Lightning Source LLC
Chambersburg PA
CBHW021430170526
45164CB00001B/175